A WORLD OF DIFFERENCE

The Home Counties
Edited by Justine Horne

Young Writers

First published in Great Britain in 2008 by:
Young Writers
Remus House
Coltsfoot Drive
Peterborough
PE2 9JX
Telephone: 01733 890066
Website: www.youngwriters.co.uk

All Rights Reserved

© Copyright Contributors 2008

SB ISBN 978-1 84431 783 7

Foreword

Young Writers' Big Green Poetry Machine is a showcase for our nation's most brilliant young poets to share their thoughts, hopes and fears for the planet they call home.

Young Writers was established in 1991 to nurture creativity in our children and young adults, to give them an interest in poetry and an outlet to express themselves. Seeing their work in print will encourage them to keep writing as they grow, and become our poets of tomorrow.

Selecting the poems has been challenging and immensely rewarding. The effort and imagination invested by these young writers makes their poems a pleasure to enjoy reading time and time again.

Contents

Neelam Shah (16)	1
Jermaine Nsubuga	1
Anthony Burnham-Marshalleck (12)	2
Hannah Wang (14)	3

Bishop Stopford's School, Enfield
Joshina McKenzie (11)	3
Armarni Griffiths (12)	4
Shaquille Uwakwe (12)	4

Boundstone Community College, Lancing
Jamie Hinkley (13)	5
Jodie Brown (13)	5
Ryan McNie (12)	6
Alexandra Stickland (13)	7
Gemma Rose (13)	7
Katie Godden (12)	8
Paula Dickerson (13)	8
Claire Louise Merritt (13)	9

Broadwater School, Godalming
Georgia Blanchard	9
Daniel Hill (12)	10
Harry Adams	10
Daniel Oakey (13)	11
Ryan Luff (13)	11
David Ewing (13)	12
Carmen Fitzmaurice	12
Zofiyah Betker (13)	13
Hannah Bush (13)	13
James Mitchell (13)	14
Hazel Fenner (13)	14
Becky Foster	15
Rosie Holcombe (11)	16
Patrick Reffell Stevens (12)	16
Chloe Shaw	17
Kalum Deacon (12)	17

Shannon Lynn (12)	18
Hannah Brown (12)	19
Laura Green (14)	19
Marissa Nash (13)	20

Coombe Girls' School, New Malden
Woosshini Sivanesakumar (13)	21

Cornfield School, Littlehampton
Joshua James Emrys-Jones (14)	21
Louisa Cuddihy (15)	22

Folkestone School for Girls, Folkestone
Ellie Hayes (13)	22
Melissa Garside (14)	23
Aimée Irving (13)	23
Natasha Wright (12)	24
Charlotte Smith (13)	25
Hannah Beale (12)	25
Rachel Talbot (14)	26
Joelle Wade (12)	26
Bethany Lennon (14)	27
Alexis Noonan (13)	27
Lauren Firmager (13)	28
Josie Dobson (14)	28
Gabrielle Bausola (14)	29
Emily Slater (14)	29
Jessica Smith (14)	30
Adrienne Fudge (14)	30
Leah Wood (14)	31
Sophie Richardson (14)	32
Rimona Rai (14)	33
Chloe Harris (13)	33
Hannah Simmons (14)	34
Kim Stevens (14)	35
Suzanne Clarke (14)	36
Tara Johnson (14)	37
Kiera Ward (13)	37

Frewen College, Northiam
    Amelia Stott (13)   38
    Taylor Brewer-Hanson (14)   38
    Tom Morton (15)   39
    Connor Fentiman (13)   39
    Charlotte Hanbury (14)   39

Glenthorne High School, Sutton
    Billy Dickson (12)   40
    Robert Sharp (12)   40
    Libby Hennessy (12)   40
    Grace Connoley (12)   41
    Alex Kemp (12)   41
    Laura Barfield (12)   42

Haling Manor High School, South Croydon
    Tia Wright (12) & Georgia Conrad   42
    Stacey Nurse & Sandy Reddy (12)   43
    Fatema Miah (12)   43
    Monique Reid (12)   44
    Alicia Harden (12)   44
    Peta-Gaye Miller (12)   45
    Georgia Matthews (12)   45
    Jasmin John (12)   46

Herbert Shiner Intermediate School, Petworth
    Isabelle Mills (11)   47
    Ebony McKay (12)   48

Highdown School & Sixth Form Centre, Reading
    Molly Whiting (11)   49
    Brigid Shields (12)   49
    Georgia Mackie (11)   50
    Jessica Knight (11)   50
    Luke Jones (11)   51
    Lucy Fisher (12)   51
    Samuel Watson (12)   52
    Ryan Allen (12)   52
    Shannon Croker (12)   53
    Marcus Simpson (11)   53

Shaakilla Mahabir (11) — 54
Richard Evans (11) — 54
Louise Champion (12) — 54
Zoe Harris (12) — 55
Emily Strong (12) — 55
Vikki Harris (12) — 55
Peter Barlow (12) — 56
Sophie Martin (12) — 56
Curtis Edwards (12) — 57
Chanel Davis (12) — 57

Howard of Effingham School, Effingham
Aimée Miles (12) — 57
Alex Chamberlain (12) — 58
Matthew Penny (12) — 58
Megan Keepence (12) — 59
Nicholas Allen (11) — 60
Ellie Collins (12) — 61
Louise Smith (12) — 62
Kathryn Draper (12) — 62
Emma Roberts (12) — 63
Oliver Lazarevic (11) — 63
Eleanor Stanley (12) — 64
Gemma Grimstead (12) — 65
Hannah Bowles (12) — 66
Victoria Holloway (12) — 67
Kyra Bracey (12) — 68

John O'Gaunt School, Hungerford
Steph Wheeler (13) — 68
Lucy Hutchins (13) — 69
Dale Terry (12) — 69
Abigail Poernig (13) — 70
Holly McMordie (12) — 71
Emma Todd (13) — 72
Holly Thorne (13) — 73
Becky Horne (13) — 74

Kemnal Technology College, Sidcup
Jimmy Grainger & James Neill-Tadman (12) — 74

Oakmeeds Community College, Burgess Hill
Keeley Wheatley (12)   75
Kelly Gregory (12)   75
Katie Howard   76
Eddie Marshall (12)   76
Lucy Bennet (12)   77
Charlie Owen (12)   78
Shannon Bowles   78
Rebecca Wilson (12)   79
Ben McCreadie   79
Vicki Wootten (12)   80

St Edmund's Catholic School, Dover
Josh King (18)   81

St John's Beaumont School, Old Windsor
William Hall (12)   82
Gregory Hart (12)   83
Omar Ibrahim (12)   84
Richard Spanos (12)   85

Sir William Ramsay School, High Wycombe
Holly Claridge (12)   85
Megan Stiles (12)   86
Josh Nicholls (11)   86

Thamesview School Gravesend
Louise Church (15)   87
Chris Hutchison (13)   87

The Brakenhale School, Brackenhall
Taylor Barnard (13)   88

The Matthew Arnold School, Staines
Zoe Tate (12)   88
Shannen Fisher (12)   89
Nancy Berry (12)   89
Daniel Morris (12)   90
Rory Carroll (12)   90
Jack Smith (13)   90
Harriet Goodger (12)   91

Harvey Parsons (12)   91
Chris Cook (12)   92
Frankie Brown (12)   92
Jonathan Wells (12)   93
Rachel Hall (12)   93
Lily Butler (13)   93
Zoe High (13)   94
Lauren Griffin (12)   94
Leanne Barnes & Kerry Bunston (12)   94

The Radcliffe School, Wolverton
Trish Bangezhano (12)   95
Hannah Greig (14)   95
Joe Bulman (13)   96
Kerry Clarke (14)   96
Matthew Rogers (13)   97
Kelsie Griffin (13)   97
Jake Munn (14)   98
Eleanor Gregory (12)   99
Daniel Jones (14)   100
Ceejay Stewart (13)   101
Ryan Murphy (13)   102
Rachel Baker (12)   102
Lauren Kemp (12)   103
Melanie Small (14)   103
Josh Davey (12)   104
Dean Joce (13)   104
Amarah Saleem (12)   105
George Janes (12)   105
Peter Downing (12)   106
Chantelle Stubbings (12)   106
Tom Compton (13)   107
Megan Duke (13)   107
Taylor Hamilton (11)   107
Shannon Weir (12)   108
EJ Cooper   108
Jadine Lane (11)   109
Laura Beaton (12)   109
Ronica Nyarirangwe (11)   110
Chelcie Addis (12)   110
Luke Turner (12)   111

Matthew Downs (12)	111
Tom Lawrence (12)	112
Joshua McMillan (12)	112
Emily Boycott	113
Jamie King (12)	113
Rachael Banes	114
Jack Webster (12)	115
Stephen Reilly (12)	115
Victoria Hardwick	116

Woodbridge Park Education Service,
Tison Bailey (13)	116
Hollie Turner (14)	117
Taylor O'Brien (13)	117

The Poems

Pigeons Of A Feather

Pigeons fly to reach their destination,
Each of them worried about extinction.

As they are the only birds of their kind,
No one cares to think in their minds
To feed these poor helpless creatures,
Even though they have beautiful features.

Soon they will all slowly start to fade away,
With empty stomachs and fear of dismay.
These pigeons constantly scavenge for food,
Some search day and night, even in a bad mood.
Sadly many of them die, mostly due to starvation,
But is it the killer? No, it is us, London's population.

Pigeons fly to reach their destination,
Each of them worried about extinction.

Neelam Shah (16)

This Place

This place will be more magnificent
Than the solar system with nine planets.

This place has clever things in it,
You can hear whispers of knowledge from a wise owl.

This place is fond of England,
The clouds picture them winning the World Cup.

This place is quite violent,
It shows nature unleashing its fury with volcanoes erupting,
Earthquakes and hurricanes.

This place is quite unusual,
As you see islands moving location.

This place will soon perish
And in reincarnation appear as a shooting star!

Jermaine Nsubuga

The World Today!

My generation can be a dark, dark place
Some children of today are a disgrace
We need to cut down on this violence and crime
People getting shot or stabbed all of the time
What is really wrong with the world today?
Young ones acting bad in front of their mates
All that's left now is bad vibes and hate
Because they think it makes them big
Because they think it makes them bad
All you're doing now is blowing everything you had
A criminal record, permanent for life
Think about that when you're pulling out the knife
It really doesn't make you cool
And it doesn't give you power
Just because you take a life every other hour
24/7
Seven days a week
Every parent worried, they can barely sleep
It really isn't fair, they do things their own way
But then a decent soul will have to pay
What can start as a look
Or cussing someone's mum
Can end up with the shooting of a gun.

So I deeply mean what I say
Let's stop the violence and let's start today
It's like taking out the trash
Today is the day
Because the violence isn't right
So today we must fight
To kick the killings out of day and night!

Anthony Burnham-Marshalleck (12)

Why The War?

Bombed are bodies
Blood-caked behind shattered figures
Tears amid streaked cheeks
Pointless is this

Bombed are bodies
Turmoil is ongoing
Misery and pain daily
Pointless is this.

Hannah Wang (14)

Untitled

This is my poem for The Big Green Poetry Machine,
But here's the thing,
I can't choose.
Should I do it about the rainforests,
Or pollution?
Animals and extinction?
Poverty and litter?
War and being homeless?
Climate change?
Racism?
Recycling?
It's hard to decide,
I really don't know.
I know a bit about animals and extinction,
But not a lot.
I recycle,
I know a bit about that.
Nah.
I don't know what to do,
But I guess this is my poem,
Even if I didn't know what to do!

Joshina McKenzie (11)
Bishop Stopford's School, Enfield

Poverty

The dark, dirty place where a child has to sleep,
The long gloomy faces of those with nothing to eat,
The tears shed as another person is taken
By a most unwanted disease,
So please help to stop the disease,
They need your help.
When you see them on the news
Do not be confused, they are real.
The world community needs to care
And create a world that is fair.

Armarni Griffiths (12)
Bishop Stopford's School, Enfield

Violence

Violence, something that separates us from coming together.
Something that happens, whatever the weather.
Stopping the violence, increasing the peace,
Saving yourself on the mean streets.
Walking around with knives and guns,
It is not who you are, you should know where you're from!
Stop the violence, it is not needed,
So many lives have been conceded!

Shaquille Uwakwe (12)
Bishop Stopford's School, Enfield

War, In My Eyes

Here, there, everywhere,
The only sound you hear all day,
A gunshot around the corner,
An explosion across the street,
A million people dying
Right in front of me.

I'm living in cardboard boxes,
Begging people for food,
Playing mum to my little sister
Cos Mum and Dad are dead.

No one cares about us,
No one can really see
The pain and suffering we go through,
Please, please, help me!

No one ever helps us,
I think it's unfair!

Jamie Hinkley (13)
Boundstone Community College, Lancing

Think Green

We should go green
If not, we're just mean.

Recycle your paper,
Recycle your tins,
This is the only way
We can win.

Think of the planet,
Think of yourselves,
Recycle your stuff
Before there's nothing else!

Jodie Brown (13)
Boundstone Community College, Lancing

The Secrets Of The Jungle

An emerald city,
A forest of green,
The greatest thing you've ever seen.
Creatures lived there,
Throughout this land,
And all was fine,
But *then came Man.*

Exploring through the jungle,
Destroying as they came,
Starting fires through the peace,
Trees crashing down in flame.

It only takes one tree
To make a thousand matches.
Only takes one match
To burn a thousand trees.

The trees were burned,
Money was earned,
This destructive race was glad.
They didn't know,
Were blind to see,
That secrets could be had.

So as they carry on,
Remember this small song,
Because they will never learn,
So the secrets of the jungle,
Forever they will burn.

Ryan McNie (12)
Boundstone Community College, Lancing

Rainforest

Rainforest, rainforest,
Full of life,
From animals to plants
And even mice.

Rainforest, rainforest,
Full of pain,
Trees coming down,
Animals going insane.

Rainforest, rainforest,
Full of tears,
It has been there so many years,
Now it's turning into dust,
All because of silly us.

Alexandra Stickland (13)
Boundstone Community College, Lancing

Life Or Death

Guns are firing,
Lives are dying,
The blood is everywhere.
As long as you duck
You will have some luck
Of living for the rest of the day.
The day has gone
And you have won,
But once you leave
You won't believe
Another war has begun!

Gemma Rose (13)
Boundstone Community College, Lancing

The World Today

The world is dying,
Help us be more aware
Of the consequences of our actions.
Do you really care?

What is the matter
With society today?
How come it's extremely hot
In the middle of May?

How can you help?
Well turn off any unwanted lights
And you'll see a big difference
All of those beautiful summer nights.

This is how the story ends,
The world is now shut down, closed.
Have you realised what is happening now?
I hope you like the poem I have composed.

Katie Godden (12)
Boundstone Community College, Lancing

War

The floor is muddy, the stench is foul,
There's constant shooting as people howl.
I think of my family I left behind -
Christmases and presents, I hear laughter in my mind.
I see a soldier, gun in hand
As I crawl through, but then I hear a bang.
The world goes black, I see no more,
I gave my life up for a silly war.

Paula Dickerson (13)
Boundstone Community College, Lancing

Short But Peaceful

Pollution, war, homelessness,
Litter all around.
Happy faces, smiles,
Green grass all about.

Being happy or sad,
Happy, happy people.
No wars, *no* racism,
No litter, *no* pollution.
Stop this happening,
Stop it!

Claire Louise Merritt (13)
Boundstone Community College, Lancing

There Is A Place

There could be a place where the
Flowers wonder and the birds sing.
The wind's left humming a beautiful song.
The children's giggles echo throughout the trees
That are left swaying in a midnight dream.

'Til the colours fuse and the beauty fades,
This engaging place is rearranged.

The weed's poison is out to kill the life,
Like the flowers standing still.
The reflection in the river is a charcoal black,
The birds' singing isn't coming back,
They're far away now, danger they fear,
Who would have thought the future lies here?

The rain shattering like splintered glass,
The trees stand no more.
Unwanted treasures suffocate the scorched grass,
While they're escaping from the poor.

Georgia Blanchard
Broadwater School, Godalming

The Clouds That Hold No Rain

They are erected from lots of steel,
They are deadly and dangerous.
Like giant cigarettes they billow to the sky
The clouds they send go way up high.
These clouds of smoke have a fight,
The atmosphere is losing.
The clouds have reinforcements.
We must stop the backup,
We must help to defeat them,
Cut off their supply and bring them down.
If we do not, the apocalypse will come.
We will have to run like cheetahs,
The floods will come, the rain will fall,
The land will collapse, this is the true end.
All we must do to save our planet
Is to stop the clouds that have no rain.

Daniel Hill (12)
Broadwater School, Godalming

Our Factory Skyline

Up and up they go,
Their image protruding awkwardly
Against the lurid twilight sky.
How do the downy white clouds skid by
So peacefully over the oblivion below?
The repulsive squander is now stamped
On our skyline for all to see,
Like a smeary blotch of ink on a letter,
Or a garish stain on a crisp white sheet.
Surely our stupidity won't affect us,
Or will it?
Alas, it is our future generations who
Perhaps may receive the brunt of our misdeeds.

Harry Adams
Broadwater School, Godalming

The Lonely Polar Bear

The lonely polar bear wandered
Across the desolate Arctic land,
Like a floating cloud lost and blown away.
A cold tear came running down
The bear's face as she thought of her family,
Long since consumed by the
Fiery powers of humans.
They had taken the polar habitat,
Stripped it bare and leaving
A dark, twisted heap of waste.
She was a beautiful polar bear,
But not just any polar bear;
The last.

Daniel Oakey (13)
Broadwater School, Godalming

My Paradise

The trees stand tall
Like soldiers in battle.
One by one
They slowly come down
As I sit and watch.

The builders move in,
So I move out.
In the distance
I see the skittles slowly fall down.

I hear on the news
That the trees have all gone
And all you can see
Is miles of buildings.

One day I would like to come back
And imagine what this place once was,
But until that day,
My imaginary world has gone.

Ryan Luff (13)
Broadwater School, Godalming

Keeping It Green

We gotta think again;
The Earth's becoming sick,
Reduce your carbon footprint
And you'd better act quick.

Bleak, thick, grey smog
Could be that rank forever,
If we don't stop wasting
And get our acts together.

You know what I reckon?
It's a deadly virus, man,
We're abusing the planet,
Let's stop it whilst we can.

Saying and doing,
They're not the same.
No second chances
Cos this is no game.

Keep it green, man.

David Ewing (13)
Broadwater School, Godalming

Green Poetry

Oh, how the Earth is like a broken heart,
Torn, ripped and thrown to one side.
It bleeds from all our danger
And suffers from all the pain.
Its heart was once healthy and pure,
But now it's condemned.
Oh, what can we do?
Is it too late to help?
If only everyone could do something small,
Our Earth could be like new again.

Carmen Fitzmaurice
Broadwater School, Godalming

What Our Planet Could Become

Bees that go buzz,
Flowers that are pink,
Every day I shudder to think
Of what our planet could become.
A rubbish tip, a great big dump,
Cans and cardboard, plastic too,
That could have been recycled,
With a pair of old shoes.
But it's too late now,
The world's a wreck,
Go out to sea and stand on deck to
See the litter floating by,
With dead sea life on the side.
This is what our planet could become.
We as humans walk under the sun,
Next time think of this rhyme
And save this planet from destruction.

Zofiyah Betker (13)
Broadwater School, Godalming

White Is The Polar Bear

White is the polar bear in his icy home,
Until it melts.

Green are the trees that allow us to breathe,
Don't cut them all down.

Blue is the sky on a summer's day,
Stop the pollution, we need to see the sky.

Yellow is the sun, fiery hot,
Don't make a hole in the ozone layer, we'll fry.

A beautiful green countryside
Filled with rubbish.

Recycle the rubbish,
Keep our planet whole.

Hannah Bush (13)
Broadwater School, Godalming

The Last Polar Bear

North to south,
Pole to pole,
Not a tiger or a vole,
I'm a rare specimen,
You won't see another one,
I'm victim to factories and the gun.
It's lonely up here,
There are only birds,
For it to come to this is really just absurd.
Who do you think you are,
Pushing me around?
You can't just find my ancestors
In the lost and found.
I really don't believe you,
Killing all my friends,
Just think, in a few years it will be the end.
I'm the last polar bear,
So spare a thought for me,
Please don't let my only home melt into the sea.

James Mitchell (13)
Broadwater School, Godalming

Pollution, Destruction And Death

Pollution, destruction and death,
Animals suffer and it is our fault.
Pollution, destruction and death,
Animals suffer, this must come to a halt.
All on their own, they fight for their lives.
All on their own, this just isn't right.
So let's put a stop to it,
Let's put a stop to it now.
Pollution, destruction and death,
Come on, let's do it now.

Hazel Fenner (13)
Broadwater School, Godalming

Why Do It?

I crawl in the fresh-cut grass,
But I want it to last.
When the wind blowed,
The river always flowed,
Ti doesn't now,
So it makes me feel down.
It makes the world feel dull,
Like when animals can't have their foals.
The rubbish is clogging up everywhere,
This is not very fair.
The big, coloured trees are bright,
But then they go bare and have no life.
They look like scarecrows being dressed,
I don't like that as they never look their best.
I can never look into the river and stare,
As I just see rubbish, such as mouldy old pears.
My friends can't have a say
As humans don't act the same way.
Polar bears are being killed
Because of the rubbish on the melted ice fields.
People need to do something quick and fast,
As everyone will have an unforgettable past.
So take time to stop and think,
Before everything goes out in a blink!

Becky Foster
Broadwater School, Godalming

Recycle, Recycle

Recycle, recycle,
Make our world a better place.

Recycle, recycle,
Rubbish taking over our ground.

Recycle, recycle,
We need more space.

Recycle, recycle,
Take a look please, a good look around.

Recycle, recycle,
If we don't, we'll regret.

Recycle, recycle,
Let us never forget.

Please stop, everyone,
Before our world is gone.

Rosie Holcombe (11)
Broadwater School, Godalming

Untitled

Billowing, black, beastly smoke,
Towering chimneys like mountains.
The buildings are giant planet-killers,
Wildlife dying at all angles.

Patrick Reffell Stevens (12)
Broadwater School, Godalming

In History, Yet Presently

In history, lakes were wonderful places
For picnics and a summer's day.
Presently, lakes are like lumpy porridge
Since masses of litter and half-full packets
Swarm the streams.

Once, a tall child's adventure, with alluring, crisp leaves.
Presently a coat hanger for plastic bags and newspapers.

In history, wide paths for vehicles were immaculate
And a pleasant place to walk beside.
Presently they are unpleasant parts of streets,
Since waste covers the edges.

Presently we are unclenching our hands to drop an item
We no longer wish to keep.
In future, only your relatives will regret it for you.

Chloe Shaw
Broadwater School, Godalming

Recycle Poem

Landfill sites like villages
Taking up the land,
All the poor little animals
Getting caught up in all our trash.

When finished with a bottle,
Don't throw it in the can,
Try to reuse it again,
That's our recycling plan.

Reduce a lot of your items
When going to the shop,
Don't throw it in the bin,
Try to recycle it again.

Kalum Deacon (12)
Broadwater School, Godalming

Trash

When the world first began,
The Garden of Eden, home to the world's first people,
Was smooth and clean and fresh,
But now it's overrun by trash.

When the Egyptians and the Romans ruled,
They kept their world pristine.
Their pyramids and armour were spotless,
But now it's ruled by trash.

The medieval people crowded the streets,
Their towns were full and busy.
The countryside was spacious and empty,
But now trash crowds the streets.

Tudor kings and queens were next,
Henry started the latest fashion - beheading - ooh, how humane.
What a shame for his six wives.
But our latest fashion is trash.

For the Victorians, they planned the future bright,
Big ideas and schemes.
Factories started, pollution was born,
But the only thing in our future is trash.

Modern days are going through rough times,
No one cares, they just carry on
Doing what they know is wrong,
Living in their trash.

If other ages could do it,
Keep their world clean,
Why can't we?
Because we're trash.

Shannon Lynn (12)
Broadwater School, Godalming

Earth's Pain

Such a peaceful world of nature is coming to the end,
Only us to make it worse and only nature to defend.
The world is overflowing,
Such a horrific scene to see,
All we can imagine is lots of greenery
Being covered by rubbish.
God's creation is no longer there,
Makes your heart feel spacious, empty and bare.
The animals are decreasing,
One by one each day,
Makes you feel unthoughtful and the words you disobey.
Rubbish floats around
The streets, parks and keeper's ground.
Think of how you could save our home
And not make it feel unknown.
Just by doing something small,
You could save us all!

Hannah Brown (12)
Broadwater School, Godalming

A Human's Planet

The sea may be rising, the planet may be warm,
But humanity has broken, our respect is gone.
Deforestation causes species to fade,
We hunt too much before more can be made.

Birds fly above in the polluted sky,
'Super race' humans live by that lie.
The seas are over-fished, the whales are gone,
This may be the end of their beautiful song.

The rubbish in the seas causes total devastation,
Few people want to help, we have no dedication.
People don't understand, we only have one chance
To look after the land, the animals and plants.

Laura Green (14)
Broadwater School, Godalming

Cause And A Consequence

P ollution is caused by us
O ur fault, our problem
L ittering is one cause
L ow level mess has high consequences
U nder lies the real damage
T housands of years' worth of mess
I n the air, ground, sea and water
O n the great seas and lakes
N o one can make a change but us

A nd we should care
N o one knows how bad it really is
D estruction is everywhere

R eal actions have real consequences
E verywhere around us
C ool ice lands melting away
Y ou could walk, what's the fuss?
C ans, paper, can all be recycled
L ots of people need to help the problem that's appearing
I n every single country
N ever forget green lands are disappearing
G o and help to make a difference.

Marissa Nash (13)
Broadwater School, Godalming

Poverty

You have no food and no shelter,
Tomorrow you may die of starvation.

If you are born into a family who are living in poverty,
It is your worst nightmare,

Begging for food every day,
Sleeping in the open street,

You have no home,
You have no place to call yours.

A life of poverty is a rare dream,
No one wants you.

You smell of sweat,
You are covered in dirt,

Your only way to survive is to steal and to murder,
You have no other choice.

For you, death is like a miracle,
Death is your only hope out of this nightmare.

Woosshini Sivanesakumar (13)
Coombe Girls' School, New Malden

Water, We Are The Same People

As the milky, murky water touches my lips,
I black out, fall to the ground and see an eclipse.
What is it like, drinking pure, clear water?
I laugh, I dance, I sing and I prance,
We have nothing valuable to fight over,
Except the love we have for each other.
As I sit in my bath, I waste water, but I laugh,
Even though I do not know I am killing people slowly.
We make bread out of water and dough.
What I don't know is how lucky we are,
To sit in a car, to waste water and drink wine,
La-di-la-di-la.

Joshua James Emrys-Jones (14)
Cornfield School, Littlehampton

When Will This War End?

I hear the little girl crying.
My mum is sighing,
Her hands are on her head.
All she wants to do is stay in bed.
Planes flying overhead,
Bombs being dropped,
Devastation all around,
Bodies scattered on the ground.
Sadness in her heart,
Waiting for a new start.
I tell myself I'll be OK,
It's only just another day.
Wanting and needing,
Crying and pleading,
When will this war end?
Why can't it just be pretend?

Louisa Cuddihy (15)
Cornfield School, Littlehampton

The Rainforest

The animals run while the sun is dawning,
The chainsaw is coming with no warning.
The trees fall down like harmless giants,
Then out pour the innocent clients.
The monstrous chainsaw chops them thin,
But the petrified animals haven't done anything!
The trees are down like dominoes,
When is it going to stop? No one knows.
The trees are falling, drop, drop, drop,
The chainsaw is chopping, chop, chop, chop.
These poor animals need to be loved,
But into a foreign zoo they are shoved.
A bit of money you could give,
This will help the animals live!

Ellie Hayes (13)
Folkestone School for Girls, Folkestone

Only An Action

Poverty isn't just a word or thought,
It's a place,
So unkempt and hungry for life.
It's a person
That doesn't even have the
Bare essentials to live.
It's the animals that have to put up with
The hunger and despair.
It's the home that houses
Many families in one bare room.
It's the terror behind their eyes
That shows the shaking mind
Of an orphan child.
The signs are there,
Glaring like the sun above,
But only a kind action
Will show them love.

Melissa Garside (14)
Folkestone School for Girls, Folkestone

Humans

H ave no emotion
U ndermining animals
M aking them feel unsafe
A gainst helping others
N ever listening, always talking
S topping our Earth from being peaceful.

Humans are stopping the world
From becoming a better place.
Give to a local charity and help.

Aimée Irving (13)
Folkestone School for Girls, Folkestone

Extinction

Swinging through the trees,
Falling to its knees,
Another orang-utan is gone.
Global warming's job is done.

Cute and cuddly, sweet to see,
Chopped down over there is its tree.
Its habitat, home, its place to stay,
Extinction is near, what's left to say?

The solution is clear,
It is true, though hard to hear.
Recycling is the way
To help orang-utans stay.

Global warming is a riddle,
No one knows just how it fiddles
With the lives of other beings.
People have just begun seeing
What a mess it makes,
All the lives it takes.

Swinging through the trees,
Falling to its knees,
Another orang-utan is gone.
Global warming's job is done!

Natasha Wright (12)
Folkestone School for Girls, Folkestone

Bullet

A contradiction of feelings,
Bang!
An innocent person is bleeding.
Devastation and destruction wherever you turn,
Will stubborn politicians ever learn?
Wars are caused by the words of men,
But can be stopped by the stroke of a peaceful pen.
A family ripped apart by the beckons of war,
A father traumatised by sights he saw.
How far will people go
To let the world know
That they are right and we are wrong?
How long will the fighting go on?

Charlotte Smith (13)
Folkestone School for Girls, Folkestone

Litter Madness

You see bins scattered everywhere,
But you really just don't care.
Go ahead, drop it on the ground
Amongst the heap of others around.

You see chewing gum on the floor,
But get yours out and drop some more.
People work to keep streets clean,
But what's the point if you are not keen?

Do you realise what you're doing?
The environment you are going to ruin.
You should really do your best
To keep the countryside picturesque.

It's a simple task
And that's all we ask.
You can change now,
We'll show you how.

Hannah Beale (12)
Folkestone School for Girls, Folkestone

Racism

Why does it matter about the colour of your skin?
Ditch this life of racism and let everybody win.
We are all humans together, who all think the same,
Anyone who is racist should hang their head in shame.
Black,
White,
Why start a fight?
We need to end racism and make it right!

Rachel Talbot (14)
Folkestone School for Girls, Folkestone

Reduce, Reuse, Recycle

Reduce, reuse, recycle,
Reduce, reuse, recycle,
Plastic, glass and paper,
Reduce, reuse, recycle.

Plastic is used for certain things,
Like bottles, bags and pots.
These items can be reused
By recycling lots and lots.

Glass is a clever one
That can be shaped in different sizes.
Recycling this one too
Can give you lots of prizes.

Paper comes from trees
Thinly sliced and cut.
Reusing this can give you more
And saves the squirrel's hut.

Reduce, reuse, recycle,
Reduce, reuse, recycle,
Plastic, glass and paper,
Reduce, reuse, recycle.

Joelle Wade (12)
Folkestone School for Girls, Folkestone

Save Our Earth

Our world is slowly heating up,
Our sea levels are rising,
Not everyone knows about the effects,
They are disturbing and surprising.

It's the little things that help the most,
Like recycling your old junk.
Things like this will help small islands,
So in years to come they're not sunk.

We need your help to save our Earth
For the generations that follow.
People are acting selfishly and mean,
As if they are just hollow.

Save our Earth
And do it now,
To save every animal,
From eagle to cow.

Bethany Lennon (14)
Folkestone School for Girls, Folkestone

Rainforest

Rainforests are light, they're also bright.
The sun is high up in the sky,
It is home, never alone.
The jungle floor, it's a total bore,
The treetops move in the groove.
The animals crash, while monkeys dash,
Parrots squawk like the hawks.
Monkeys squeak, the jungle is bleak,
The colours shine, all pretty in a line.
Life is mad, but it's turning sad.

Alexis Noonan (13)
Folkestone School for Girls, Folkestone

War Is Bad

Young men dying out there,
Losing their lives, surely that's not fair.
Bombs, swords, planes and tanks,
We owe them a lot of thanks.

When they go, they leave their families,
Travelling across many seas.
The long, anxious journey there,
All they can do is sit and stare.

Many may lose their lives,
Losing children, husbands and wives,
Fathers, brothers, sisters, mothers,
Not forgetting all the others.

But some may fly back home safe,
Throughout the war, they keep their faith.
Let's help to end this war,
Because it's something we've been waiting for.

Lauren Firmager (13)
Folkestone School for Girls, Folkestone

The Brown World

The sky was blue and now it's brown,
There's a big hole in the ozone layer.
The grass was green and fresh but now it's limp and dead,
There's a big hole in the ozone layer.
The plants used to grow tall but now they're weak and small,
There's a big hole in the ozone layer.
The sea used to be a lovely scene and now it is a dirty green,
There's a big hole in the ozone layer.
The seasons are never consistent and we need to be persistent,
There's a big hole in the ozone layer.
The world is gradually falling apart because of our laziness,
Because we need to fix the big hole in the ozone layer.

Josie Dobson (14)
Folkestone School for Girls, Folkestone

Abuse

You see a young girl walking down the street,
Nothing really special but she seems sweet,
But do you really know what happens behind closed doors,
Where she's kicked, punched and bullied and made to do chores?

She doesn't complain and she doesn't moan,
But she trembles with fear when her father comes home.

She gets scared and frightened when she's alone
And wants to tell someone, but can't pick up the phone.
She's scared of what her father might do,
And she's scared for her life and her brother's too.

If she cried out for help would you even care?
Would you walk on by, or stop and stare?
Would you help her and tell her that everything's all right,
Or leave her to suffer another unbearable night?

Ask yourself the question, is it really fair,
And if you knew her, would you care?

Gabrielle Bausola (14)
Folkestone School for Girls, Folkestone

Save The Animals, Before Time Runs Out!

From seals, snow leopards and bears, they take
Their fur and fancy fur coats they make.
Wonderful animals that live in the sea
Are taken, and for their blubber, people pay a great fee.

Rubbish is thrown out on the street,
Kicked about by people's feet.
The litter around pollutes the Earth,
Ruining the animals' habitat, their turf.

Within a few years they'll all disappear,
There will be no happiness, no bright cheer.
We need to help them now, we need to help them fast,
So come quickly please, before the animals of this world
Become a thing of the past.

Emily Slater (14)
Folkestone School for Girls, Folkestone

A Black And White World

Everyone is equal,
Everyone should be treated the same,
But to some heartless people,
This is just a game.

What's so wrong with black people?
They're just the same as you and me.
Why do some people hate them?
Why do they hang them on trees?

People are killed because of their skin colour,
Families are forced out,
But no one hears their cries for help,
No one hears their shouts.

Black people deserve happy lives too,
They've done nothing wrong.
This world needs to unite as one,
And make racism gone.

Jessica Smith (14)
Folkestone School for Girls, Folkestone

Girl In Poverty

She has no food,
Her feet are bare,
She has no other clothes to wear.

Her skin is fragile,
Her hair is limp,
Her face is absent of a smile.

She has no money,
Education or home,
It seems as if she is all alone.

A little money could go a long way,
So why not give
So she can start her life again today?

Adrienne Fudge (14)
Folkestone School for Girls, Folkestone

It Can Only Be War

The sound of gunshots ringing in my ears,
The sound of crying men frozen in my mind,
The scene of death strewn about my feet,
It can only be war.

It's now pitch-black and my friends lay dead,
I walk on alone, my gun on my back,
No path to follow,
It can only be war.

I haven't written home yet, they probably think I am dead,
I feel so alone here, the only ones that are with me
Are the ones that are dead.
It can only be war.

I have killed many people today.
The guilt is unbearable.
I am a murderer, I am in sin.
It can only be war.

When will it be over?
I decided it's when I choose.
I have had enough of this murderous wasteland,
I hold the gun to my head.
It can only be death.

Leah Wood (14)
Folkestone School for Girls, Folkestone

War Is All Around

War happens all around,
Not just on the ground,
In the sea and in the sky.
People live and people die.

Some people feel grief and loss,
Others just don't give a toss.
When in war soldiers just don't care
About keeping to the rules or playing fair.

Grenades, missiles, bombs and guns,
Women losing husbands and sons.
Trucks, planes, ships and tanks,
Soldiers moving up the ranks.

Bangs and crashes driving people mad,
How did it ever get this bad?
Will the countries' problems mend?
Will this war ever end?

Together we can make this right,
Without having to start a fight.
Together we can end this war
Without bending or breaking the law.

Sophie Richardson (14)
Folkestone School for Girls, Folkestone

Colour Of Skin

Abuse, attack,
All for what?
For nothing but the colour of their skin.

Sensitive, sorrowful,
Building up within.
Self-conscious on the outside,
Dying on the inside.

Criticised, crying,
That's gone too far.
Without a doubt,
This is just too much.

Racism, riots,
They've got to be stopped.
Do you really think it's worthwhile?

Rimona Rai (14)
Folkestone School for Girls, Folkestone

Speak Out

Weeks and months go by without a meal to eat
So you wake up hungry.
Without clean water, life's not at its full,
Without education there's no way out for them,
Without a place to call home, sleep is rare.
You can be that person.
Why not speak out?

Chloe Harris (13)
Folkestone School for Girls, Folkestone

Forgotten

Now I'm dead,
I lie here,
Caught in the crossfire,
Forgotten.
My only purpose,
To remind those alive
Of the terrors of war.

Now I'm dead
I will lie here
To the end of the war,
Forgotten.
They won't find me.
I found a place no one can find,
But a bomb detected my presence.

Now I'm dead,
I lie here
Thinking about those I love,
But forgotten,
For they think I'm alive.
I dread their faces
When the death letter arrives.

Now I'm dead,
I lie here
Thinking of when this war is over
And forgotten.
The land and people will be scarred,
But I hope
They all move on in peace.

Now I'm dead,
I lie here,
Respected as a hero of the dead war,
No longer forgotten.

Hannah Simmons (14)
Folkestone School for Girls, Folkestone

It's Time For A Change

We all live in this world,
All living the same way,
But treated differently,
Without any say.

Walking down the street
You get that look
Like you have done something wrong.
The look people give to taunt you.

Living our normal lives
We are all the same.
Surrounding population of people
Who are joining in on the life game.

Being treated differently gets us down,
Only because of the skin we have.
Some people can't get jobs,
So they have to live in a public lav.

This is not fair,
This is not right,
We are all the same,
It's time to put up a fight.

It's time for a change
In all of the planet.
Everyone should be happy,
And anyone that is racist should just can it!

Kim Stevens (14)
Folkestone School for Girls, Folkestone

A War Through Time

A war through time, caught in our sight,
With it came change and endless plight.
Roman conquest as religions surely spread,
The decline of Rome, Vikings instead.

1066 Normandy, with it brought
The feudal system, a government sought.
Knighthood to proceed, lands in France,
All of this hunted, unfound by chance.

Expanses of money bought new lands,
The 100 Years War, violence out of hand.
Opportunities of the renaissance, civil wars,
Industries boom and territory soars.

World War I and World War II,
Bigger and better, by now, what's new?
Religion, land, differences and space,
Cold war, governments, a power race.

The future is what history holds,
Terrorism, weapons, nuclear in bold.
Richer countries dominate the poor,
Poverty increases from debts before.

It's always been the same, out of hand,
The higher powers' say will forever stand.

Suzanne Clarke (14)
Folkestone School for Girls, Folkestone

Let Our Rainforests Be

Don't kill our animals,
Don't cut down our trees,
Don't increase global warming,
Let our rainforests be.

Protect our endangered species,
It's in the hands of you and me.
Grow sustainable rainforests,
Let our rainforests be.

The diversity of the birdlife,
It's a wonder to be seen,
Keep for future generations,
Let our rainforests be.

They remove carbon dioxide,
So our air remains clean.
Don't destroy these habitats,
Let our rainforests be!

Tara Johnson (14)
Folkestone School for Girls, Folkestone

Jungle

Animals running around in the wild
Human beings, not even a child.

Lion cubs running around
Dirty paws touching the ground

Tall trees like dominoes, *bang, bang, bang!*
Sound from the chainsaws, *clang, clang, clang!*

> Now the jungle is silent
> Now, no life is left . . .

Kiera Ward (13)
Folkestone School for Girls, Folkestone

Animals And Extinction: Tigers

Wild endangered animals will be no more,
While their fur is on your floor.
The tiger's orange fur and black stripes are divine,
Especially out in the bright sunshine.
The tiger's roar is very mighty,
You shouldn't take its survival lightly.
Tigers are still living creatures, for crying out loud,
So you shouldn't spill their blood to get a crowd.
To have no tigers is like a meadow with no green,
We should help the tigers before they're no longer seen.
The tiger's death tastes like blood so sour,
To see their dawn with no more mighty power.
To have no tigers is like having no imagination,
Just a white blank along with our concentration.

Amelia Stott (13)
Frewen College, Northiam

Racism

Racism is a very bad thing,
It can be about the colour of the skin.
Martin Luther King had a great big dream,
Racism is a very bad thing,
Racism can be about different things,
Racism is bad and no one wins,
Racism is a very bad thing.
Racism comes in many different forms,
It can destroy your life like a great big storm.
Racism is a very bad thing.

Taylor Brewer-Hanson (14)
Frewen College, Northiam

Common Zen

It came through
The open windows
On a cold
Summer's evening,
An expected breeze.
You sent the sun round the yard, my love,
You were in the trees as the birds sang their song,
You were in the lake where the fish come from,
You were there for the branch that fell
And left its home of strength.
You are my Earth.

Tom Morton (15)
Frewen College, Northiam

Living On The Street

We're all on the street
Struggling to eat,
Only way I survive
Is if I go out thieving.
But then I get caught.
It's the outside world I'm leaving.
At least if I'm inside
I'll have shelter from the rain
And maybe some help to release my pain.

Connor Fentiman (13)
Frewen College, Northiam

Animals In Extinction

Pandas, like big fluffy toys in the sunshine,
Their black and white fur is divine.
We need more people to free them from chaos,
Desperation and pollution.
There really could be some solution.

Charlotte Hanbury (14)
Frewen College, Northiam

Restless Rainforest

Why cut our rainforests down?
Would you like us to destroy your local town?
You will regret chopping our trees one day,
When the planet's all brown and grey.
The weather s getting hot,
But you just stand and watch us rot.

Billy Dickson (12)
Glenthorne High School, Sutton

Trees, Air And Earth

The trees, the air and now the Earth,
How could you do this to us?
What have the trees done to deserve this?
The air, how could you pollute it? Now we choke.
Earth the place we live,
If that is destroyed then we become extinct.
Please, please help make our world a better, safer place!

Robert Sharp (12)
Glenthorne High School, Sutton

Nature Is Green

Nature is green,
It is the springtime
In a recycling bin.
It can be sunny or rainy.
Nature is a pair of wellies,
A muddy, murky pond,
A mundane documentary,
A green piece of grass.

Libby Hennessy (12)
Glenthorne High School, Sutton

Animal Cruelty

My eyes are sore,
My paws are weak,
My tail is no more,
My coat isn't sleek.

It's a constant duel,
My owners are cruel,
They deprive me of food,
Why are they so rude?

With fear I yelp,
Crying for help,
I prick up my ears
But nobody hears.

Slowly I die
As I solemnly cry.
My heart has stopped,
My head has flopped.

Grace Connoley (12)
Glenthorne High School, Sutton

The Boy Who Said War

Death and destruction,
That's all I can see.
War on Earth,
Is that all there will be?
I'm twelve years old
And holding a gun,
Forced into the army,
It isn't much fun.
In a few seconds
A bomb will go off
And the Earth shall feel
Humanity's wrath.

Alex Kemp (12)
Glenthorne High School, Sutton

Litter

Litter, litter everywhere,
People in our world just don't care.
We are given recycling bins,
So recycle cardboard, plastic and tins.
What is this world coming to?
We all need to break through.

Laura Barfield (12)
Glenthorne High School, Sutton

The Carbon Footprint

White is for stress
And soon this world will be a mess
If we don't strive to stick together,
Then what will happen to the weather?

The world is absolutely falling apart
Because we have a very hard heart.
This can be really easy as eating a pie,
But instead you want us all to die.

This can take years,
So forget about those gears.
We all need to communicate
So we can appreciate.

Make your carbon footprint small
By not watching TV at all,
By saving energy in every way,
By caring about our world
Every single day!

Tia Wright (12) & Georgia Conrad
Haling Manor High School, South Croydon

The Carbon Footprint In Response

I really don't believe in carbon footprints.
Humans are so insensitive, they don't have a clue.

I think I'll drive my car today . . .
It's my time to pollute and shine.

We are so innovative, we are the best.
I'm in the making of destroying this planet!

If carbon footprints exist, they aren't smart.
I am an evil genius (mm, wuh, ha ha).

I have switched off my carbon footprint.
Yeah, he switched off the TV.

We humans control everything.
Those humans allow us to dominate the world.

We'll chase away those carbon footprints.
With the state of this world, we aren't going anywhere!

Stacey Nurse & Sandy Reddy (12)
Haling Manor High School, South Croydon

The Carbon Footprint

The carbon footprint is black,
It sounds like a squashed bug,
It tastes like bitter fruit,
It looks like a muddy stain,
It smells like a dirty sock.

We should all work together
To reduce the amount of carbon we produce,
To make the world a better place.
To make the world a much better place!

Fatema Miah (12)
Haling Manor High School, South Croydon

The Environment

The world is like a falling plane
About to hit the ground.
You can prevent the plane from crashing
By not making junk-filled mounds.

The world is like a football
Being kicked around the place.
You can reduce your carbon footprint
By doing things that aren't a disgrace.

The environment is our home - keep it clean.
The environment is our land - keep it green.
The environment is our soil - plant what you need.
The environment is our Earth - plant a seed.

Monique Reid (12)
Haling Manor High School, South Croydon

The Carbon Footprint

Everyone is talking about it.
Did you hear?
The carbon footprint is here to fear!

Just to hear everyone talking about it
Sends shivers down my spine,
There is no going back in time.

So listen well,
Because this is not a joke,
This thing in the air
Will make you choke,

Everyone is talking about it,
What are you going to do
To reduce your carbon
Footprint too?

Alicia Harden (12)
Haling Manor High School, South Croydon

You Wonder Why

When you're homeless, you feel alone,
No family, no friends, no feline to share a bone.
You wonder why the world has brought you here,
With creeping murderers and burglars who scare.

Every night you wonder why,
You feel a deep hole in your heart, making you cry.
You feel like the world is falling apart.
No one to look out for you, they have no heart.

You hide behind the dustbin, taking cover.
Why? You hear a screeching noise creeping closer.
To live on the streets, how long can you survive?
Will the world live longer? How long will you be alive?

Peta-Gaye Miller (12)
Haling Manor High School, South Croydon

Saving The Environment

We are the world and it is falling apart
Because of its artery-blocked heart.
The smell, the smog, the rubbish-filled streets,
The hot, humid air and the melting ice meet.

So use up your energy to save the world,
Every man, woman, boy and girl,
Get up and start recycling today,
Build for the future, we're here to stay.

Georgia Matthews (12)
Haling Manor High School, South Croydon

Carbon Emissions

Make yourself carbon-free today,
Offset your carbon emissions for a year,
Want to keep our world clear?
Now is the time to face your fear!

Make your family carbon free,
Offset your carbon emissions for a year,
No need for tears,
It's time for cheers!

Make your car carbon free,
Offset your carbon emissions for a year,
Always listen with both ears
And I'll say it again so that you hear.

Have to fly?
Make your flight carbon free,
Offset your carbon emissions for a year,
Come and plant a tree!

Show just how much you care,
Stop stripping this world bare!

Jasmin John (12)
Haling Manor High School, South Croydon

Ruined Rainforest

The air is hot and humid,
The trees block out the sun,
Creatures creep and crawl,
Slither, slide and run.

Monkeys swing from branch to branch,
Birds fly in the sky,
Swooping, soaring, singing their song,
Flying free and high.

Leopards creep through scrub and ferns
Hunting for their prey,
Stalking, slinking, jumping out,
That monkey just got away.

Then new animals came,
Like none we've ever seen,
Tearing down the trees and bushes,
Roaring through the green.

They scared off the animals,
The birds all flew away,
The metal monster ripped apart
Everything in its way.

We used to be free,
This was our home,
But now they've destroyed everything
And made it all their own.

Isabelle Mills (11)
Herbert Shiner Intermediate School, Petworth

Rainforest Animals

Some of us are big,
Some of us are small,
But if you keep cutting down trees,
There won't be any of us at all.

We come in a range of colours,
From red to green to yellow,
We often are quite happy,
If you cut down trees, we feel rather mellow.

Some like day,
Some like night,
You humans tend to give us
Such a fright.

Some live in trees,
Others live on the ground,
Some of us are quite loud,
Others don't make a sound.

We are the rainforest animals,
So stop cutting down trees
Because you are ruining our home
And we don't like it!

Ebony McKay (12)
Herbert Shiner Intermediate School, Petworth

Go Green!

Go green,
Don't be mean.
Don't be red,
Red is dead!

Go green,
Go green.
Don't be mean,
You will feel better.

Go green,
Our world will be clean!
Recycle paper,
Please don't be a traitor.

Go green,
Go green.
Don't be mean,
You will feel better.

Molly Whiting (11)
Highdown School & Sixth Form Centre, Reading

Green Mean Machine

Go green, don't be mean,
Keep our world clean
Like a baked bean.

Recycle a bicycle and a plane,
Never ever forget your name.

Rubbish here, recycling there,
I can't bear.
Red is mean,
Like a *teen*.

Go green, go green,
Keep our planet clean!

Brigid Shields (12)
Highdown School & Sixth Form Centre, Reading

Think Green

Go green, don't be mean!
Go green, don't be mean!

Crisp packets all over the floor,
It should be against the law.
Think of the world as a better place,
So run to school in a race.

Go green, don't be mean!
Go green, don't be mean!

Don't go to school in a car,
And don't drop cans from the bar.

Go green, don't be mean!
Go green, don't be mean!

Georgia Mackie (11)
Highdown School & Sixth Form Centre, Reading

Green And Clean

Can we make
The planet green?
Can we stop pollution
And be clean?

Would you make
The planet green?
Could you stop pollution
And be clean?

Let's all make
The planet green.
Let's all stop pollution
And be clean.

Have a green life
And a clean life.

Jessica Knight (11)
Highdown School & Sixth Form Centre, Reading

Loving Greater

Go green, don't be mean,
Go green, don't be red,
Wake up now, get out of bed.

Break something, like something,
Break something, like something,
Love something greater.

We want to know why it is so,
We want to know what you would love,
To fly up high like a dove.
Red is low, it's got to go,
Go green and walk across a rainbow.
Love something greater!

Luke Jones (11)
Highdown School & Sixth Form Centre, Reading

Go Green And Think

Go green, go green,
Everyone is going green.
Think of the pollution,
We need to find a solution.

Go green, go green,
The climate is changing,
And the rainforest needs to stay.
Homeless need homes.
Go green, go green,
Stop and think.

Go green and *think!*

Lucy Fisher (12)
Highdown School & Sixth Form Centre, Reading

Green Planet Through The Fire And The Flames

The Honda came to Earth from a mighty comet,
Tearing up our roads
And now the Earth is rotting.
Polar bears are dying,
Our grandchildren may be crying.

Now a man has stepped out of the shadows
And he won't give up trying.
Half the world is crying
Because mothers and children are dying.

He woke up in the morning,
Opened up the curtains,
He got on his bike
Cos humanity is frying.
Someone on this planet
Knows how to save the world.

He took over after extinction and the litter,
And now he is king of the world.

Samuel Watson (12)
Highdown School & Sixth Form Centre, Reading

Don't Let The Ice Melt

Go green, don't be mean,
Make our world a better place.
Make there be weather we expect.
Don't let the ice melt,
Don't let the ice melt,
Don't let pollution destroy our lives,
We won't live in worry,
So don't let the ice melt,
Don't let the ice melt.

Ryan Allen (12)
Highdown School & Sixth Form Centre, Reading

The Green Bean

Go green,
Be a bean,
Shout 'n' scream,
Be eco-friendly
To The Big Green Poetry Machine.

Recycle your rubbish
So you can use it again.
Instead of using your car, walk everywhere,
Then you won't pollute the air.

Go green,
Be a bean,
Shout 'n' scream,
Be eco-friendly
To The Big Green Poetry Machine.

Go green today,
Then we won't have to pay
For the damage we cause every day.

Shannon Croker (12)
Highdown School & Sixth Form Centre, Reading

Recycle, Recycle

Recycle bottles,
Recycle cans,
Don't throw them or you'll be banned.
Recycle, recycle.

Don't throw rubbish on the ground,
Pick it up and you'll be crowned.
Recycle, recycle.

Use less cars,
Use more buses,
Don't waste petrol,
Keep it clean.
Recycle, recycle.

Marcus Simpson (11)
Highdown School & Sixth Form Centre, Reading

Our World Needs Our Help

Green, green poetry machine,
Our world needs our help.
Green, green poetry machine,
How do you think we felt?

Green, green poetry machine,
We need to stop this pollution.
Green, green poetry machine,
We need to find a solution!

Shaakilla Mahabir (11)
Highdown School & Sixth Form Centre, Reading

Dead Earth

Tramps dropping dead on the street,
Eating litter and glitter.
There's a war on over animals,
All because of poverty.
Climate change and the ozone layer
Causing the ice caps to melt.

Richard Evans (11)
Highdown School & Sixth Form Centre, Reading

Go Green!

Go green, save trees,
Be clean, no litter dropped,
We are the only ones to blame
For the dreaded climate change.

Don't chop down nature's home
Or all the animals will live alone.
If we pollute, nature's life is dying,
So go green and show you care.

Louise Champion (12)
Highdown School & Sixth Form Centre, Reading

Save The Rainforest

Everybody, he was cutting the trees,
He was fast like the monkey.
Everybody, he was just so wild
And angry like the crocodile.

Those people are so mean,
They really are.
Think about the animals,
Just don't go too far!

Zoe Harris (12)
Highdown School & Sixth Form Centre, Reading

Eco-Kids

Go green, go green,
Don't be mean.
Think about
When you put the rubbish out.
Go green, go green,
Scream and shout
When you put the rubbish out.
Go green, go green!

Emily Strong (12)
Highdown School & Sixth Form Centre, Reading

Everyone Deserves A Second Chance!

Go green, go green,
Don't be so mean,
Give it a chance,
Go green, go green.

Everyone deserves a second chance,
Depending on what they do.
Have you ever smelt
All the rubbish on the floor?

Vikki Harris (12)
Highdown School & Sixth Form Centre, Reading

Hey You!

Hey you!
Listen to me
Because I've got something to say . . .

Recycle your waste,
With haste,
Or the world will be a wasted place.

Seas growing,
Rivers flooding,
Forests shrinking,
Animals dying,
Children crying.

Hey you! Yes you,
It's not too late,
Please don't wait,
Don't let it all go wrong.

Peter Barlow (12)
Highdown School & Sixth Form Centre, Reading

Go Green And Save The World

Go to green from red,
Recycle your paper,
Your glass
And your paper boxes,
Save a tree's life.
Go to green from red,
Don't put your rubbish anywhere,
Put it in the bin.
Walk to town,
Let your car collect dust.
Go to green from red.

Sophie Martin (12)
Highdown School & Sixth Form Centre, Reading

Make It A Green Day

Make it a green day,
Don't delay,
This is what I say,
We should not have a red day.

Curtis Edwards (12)
Highdown School & Sixth Form Centre, Reading

Let's Go Green

Go green, go green,
Don't be a bean
And don't be mean.
Recycling is not hard.
The grass is covered in rubbish,
We need to stop the pollution,
We need to make a solution
For this pollution.

Chanel Davis (12)
Highdown School & Sixth Form Centre, Reading

Litter Is There . . .

We need loads more bins,
We need to do something about it,
We need to change this.

People drop litter,
People then are not helping,
People ruin it.

Countryside after,
Countryside in a big mess,
Countryside not happy.

Litter, we need to stop it!

Aimée Miles (12)
Howard of Effingham School, Effingham

Life

Trees plunging to the humid floor,
Animal cries echo through the forest.
The natural givers dying, the world burning,
Factories puffing out smoke like a raging dragon,
Killing the ozone layer, rays becoming trapped.
Ice caps disappearing like a magician,
Dirty litter choking our beaches,
Takeaway boxes clogging up the streets,
Cruel wars separating families,
Tearing apart communities, killing thousands,
The smell of burning rubble, children screaming.
But still there is hope, a light at the end of the tunnel.
Recycle and do your bit!

Alex Chamberlain (12)
Howard of Effingham School, Effingham

It's Everywhere

As I walk down the street I see it,
It's everywhere,
It's everywhere.
As I walk through the park I see it,
It's everywhere,
It's everywhere.
As I walk on the beach I see it,
It's everywhere,
It's everywhere.
It's plastic bottles and cans,
It's beer bottles and newspapers.
Litter is everywhere,
It's on all of our minds,
Except the people that don't care.

Matthew Penny (12)
Howard of Effingham School, Effingham

Litter

On the streets and in the parks,
It's everywhere I go.
Ice cream wrappers and drinks bottles,
Does it belong there? *No!*
In the middle of the roads and pavements,
Just lying upon the floor,
Crisp packets and drinks cartons,
Trampled on a little more.
Litter, like lost children,
Looking for bins.
Cigarettes and takeaway boxes,
Along with broken tins,
And do our people care?
Not a single little bit,
Making our world angry,
So here we cannot sit.
We must not stop
Until our litter is cleaned and put away,
And surely all those horrid people
Will not bear to stay.

Megan Keepence (12)
Howard of Effingham School, Effingham

I Will Put In The World . . .
(Inspired by 'Magic Box' by Kit Wright)

I will put in the world . . .
The breeze of a sailing boat,
A sight of a glider plane
And the laughter of a child on a bike.

I will put in the world . . .
The taste of an organic egg,
The smell of sweet honey
And the taste of fresh fish.

I will put in the world . . .
The sound of a car with zero emissions,
The song of a liar bird
And the sound of an uncut rainforest.

I will put in the world . . .
A happy polar bear,
A thousand new pandas
And the dodo back on Earth.

In my mind the Earth is an old football,
With green grass stains for land
And blue paint for the sea.
Put these together and it will make . . .
An eco-friendly world!

Nicholas Allen (11)
Howard of Effingham School, Effingham

I Will Take Out Of The World . . .

(Inspired by 'Magic Box' by Kit Wright)

I will take out of the world . . .
The Coke cans off the beaches,
The hunters who kill our beautiful wildlife,
The people who just don't care.

I will take out of the world . . .
All the devastating bombs in America,
The rivers chugging with pollution,
The racist thugs of our time.

I will take out of the world . . .
A homeless person who is rich,
A queen who is poor,
A mugger stealing from a pensioner.

My world is fashioned from
Fire, ice and a little curry powder.
The walls are made out of hope,
It's people who are greedy and selfish.

I shall fly in my world,
Spreading a blanket of happiness,
Taking out depression
And adding a waveful of desire.

Ellie Collins (12)
Howard of Effingham School, Effingham

Litter!

All the litter on the beaches
Scattered all over everywhere,
Bottles, paper, wrappings,
Why, oh why, oh why, no!
The Earth is being destroyed, why?
Soft sand spoiled by rubbish, but why?
Are we selfish or are we not?
Can anyone answer this?
How can we stop the climate change?
Anything is possible, so . . .
Reduce, reuse, recycle.
If we do all these things we will live.
Earth is still changing!
Now every little helps!
Just do your bit and we can change *now!*

Louise Smith (12)
Howard of Effingham School, Effingham

Climate Change - Haikus

Climate change causes
Death, destruction, disaster,
Everything bad.

Pollution caused by
Things such as greenhouse gases,
Cars and exhaust fumes.

Carbon footprint and
CO_2 imprinting on
The entire world.

Extinction of the
Animals, environments
All being destroyed.

Ice caps and deserts
And rainforests, melting,
Burning, cutting down.

Kathryn Draper (12)
Howard of Effingham School, Effingham

Litter

The litter around us is getting worse
By planting it on our Earth.
People don't care about the litter
But they'd better soon, because it's getting bitter.
Recycling could be the answer to our problems,
So could reducing and reusing,
But the things on the beach
And the things on the street
Are much worse than they used to be.
Plastic bags are drowning our fish,
Even though we eat them on a dish.
Everyone has a wish, and my wish is
For the environment never to be given retirement.

Emma Roberts (12)
Howard of Effingham School, Effingham

There Is Poverty!

The helpless face of a child
Without his family,
Looking for light.
He was as cold as an ice lolly,
As he roamed the streets of Iraq.
Ridehar's pa got taken by the Iraqi army,
The poor family got bombed in their home.
He survived but he had no money,
He was begging for more.
His clothes were doll's clothes,
All that he could find.
As he walked along, all the trees moaned and groaned.
Ridehar had given up hope,
War, war, war, it has done no good,
All that it has done
Is give innocent people no families or home.

Oliver Lazarevic (11)
Howard of Effingham School, Effingham

Our World

As a child of the world
Will I see
A squirrel on a branch,
Or a cod in the sea?

As a child of the world
Will I hear
The sound of distant guns
And the feeling of fear?

As a child of the world
Will I sleep
In a cardboard box
With no shoes for cold feet?

As a child of the world
Will I be
Taunted and hurt
By a racist community?

As a child of the world
Will I care
To help someone poor
And give all I can spare?

As a child of the world
Will I ever see
A clear blue sky
And a world smog-free?

As a child of the world
Will I burn
In a country too hot?
Or will we learn . . .

To look after our world?

Eleanor Stanley (12)
Howard of Effingham School, Effingham

What A Wonderful World . . . Or Is It?

The poor animals,
1% of them dying,
every single year.

Cutting down the trees,
They now can't sway in the wind
And can't shake my hand.

Follow the three Rs,
Reduce, reuse, recycle,
Save the planet.

In our world,
Different-coloured people
Stop being horrid.

A horrible fate
For people who go to war,
Most soldiers will die.

Oh what a sad place
In which we live now.
Let's be better fast.

Gemma Grimstead (12)
Howard of Effingham School, Effingham

Climate Change Earth

The world was happy
But we are ruining it.
We all can cure it.

Ice caps are melting,
Polar bears' homes are destroyed
Because of climate change.

Trees are cutting down,
We live on their oxygen,
We *need* them to live.

Ice caps melt
As fast as any ice cream,
It runs into the sea.

The weather is warmer
Then suddenly much colder
In the wrong seasons.

Owls' homes are lost as
Trees fall down like dominoes,
Crinkled like old men.

The world was happy
But we are ruining it.
We can all cure it.

Hannah Bowles (12)
Howard of Effingham School, Effingham

That's Just Us

We think we live in a perfect world,
A perfect country.
We don't.
Poverty, racism, war, extinction.
Over in Africa
People are dying,
Starving,
Dehydrating,
Bodies poisoned from illness . . .
But medicine comes at a cost.
To find a cure
Takes more life than the disease.
Animals
Killed for us.
Our stupidity.

Mental torture,
Physical torture
All over the world
Whilst we sleep.
We talk,
We campaign
But we don't do.
We have our cars,
Our factories,
Our world.
It was given to us.
We got our chance
And we blew it.
No one likes a bully.
We are the bullies . . .
Of the world.

Victoria Holloway (12)
Howard of Effingham School, Effingham

Polar Bear, Polar Bear

Polar bear, polar bear what do you see?
I see an iceberg melting on me.
Polar bear, polar bear what do you hear?
I hear a laugh haunting me.
Polar bear, polar bear how do you feel?
I feel like I'm sizzling on a barbecue.
Polar bear, polar bear what do you touch?
I touch the boiling water swimming around me.
Polar bear, polar bear what do you smell?
I smell the death of my friends and family.
Polar bear, polar bear what used to be?
I used to have a family beside me.
Polar bear, polar bear what do you want?
I want climate change to *stop!*

Kyra Bracey (12)
Howard of Effingham School, Effingham

Recycling, Recycling

Recycle, recycle, it's a really great thing to do,
We're saving the planet for you and you and you.
Wake up, you sleepyhead, and get out of bed,
Enjoy the day and don't waste it away.
Recycle, recycle, it's a really great thing to do,
We're saving the planet for you and you and you.
So sort out your rubbish and recycle what you can,
For it's our job to save the world and reuse things made by Man.
Recycle, recycle, it's a really great thing to do,
We're saving the planet for you and you and you.
We can reuse lots of things such as glass, paper and tins,
So take a walk and put them in the recycling bins.
Recycle, recycle, it's a really great thing to do,
We're saving the planet for you and you and you.
Recycle! So go recycle, *God bless.*

Steph Wheeler (13)
John O'Gaunt School, Hungerford

Please Recycle And Don't Litter

Get recycling bins
To throw away your tins,
It will make life better,
To write the public a letter
To show that recycling is good,
To make another childhood.

Litter, what a mess,
Love it less and less.
The bin needs to be fed
And the litter can go to bed.
The floor's on a diet,
Don't cause a riot.
Litter can kill.
You can find it on a country hill,
Where litter is thrown,
Where this isn't an animal's proper home.

Lucy Hutchins (13)
John O'Gaunt School, Hungerford

World Peace

Ride a bicycle
And always recycle.
Animals could become extinct
If you don't think.
If you forget about war,
We'll be safe, for sure.
If you stop pollution,
We'll stop execution.
If you're feeling helpless,
Come on down and help us.
If you hate litter,
Make the streets glitter.
If you're in distress,
Why don't you help the rest?

Dale Terry (12)
John O'Gaunt School, Hungerford

The Dead Earth

The Earth will die,
I can see it in my eyes,
But it will and why
It is not a lie.
Try to see and hear
And get your key.
Try to see
What you are doing to me.

Racism is wrong,
Ask them to be your friend.
Come join nations,
It is the best thing to do,
Shame we can't see how
Much pain we cause.

People are sad,
They have no homes,
They are turning mad,
They cannot get a loan.
They once had
A home!

Abigail Poernig (13)
John O'Gaunt School, Hungerford

Modern-Day Slavery

The road was aglow with firelight
Lit by the funeral lamps.
The smoke from the pyre;
A ribbon of lace,
Stained red with the desert sand.

As I sat on the ground,
My face wet with tears,
I heard a noise in the undergrowth,
And out shuffled a boy in desert clothes
That rustled and shook as he walked.

As I stared in amazement
This strange boy began to speak.
All the words were full of power
And in a language I did not know,
And yet somehow I understood.

His words were awash with beckoning.
'Come with me,' they seemed to say.
So bursting with curiosity,
I followed him away.

He led me through the desert
To a city paved with gold,
But inside these precious streets
The saddest sight I did find.

It was there that I discovered
The secret of a million poverties,
The developed world's treachery
To those penniless hordes.

Diamond mines were one cause
Of their awful state.
Employ the poor for the worst jobs, of course.
Water was poisoned, broken promises, and beatings all around.

Holly McMordie (12)
John O'Gaunt School, Hungerford

Bird's Eye View

At a quick glance the world seems fine,
But up here in the skies it's another story.
As I swoop and swirl, surfing the winds,
Down below is a jostle of bodies and buildings.

Where was once a world of peaceful happenings,
Is now a war zone, like dead man's land,
With countries at war, unresolved with fighting and sorrow,
People too scared to venture out of their homes.

I see zooming gas machines race along zigzagging roads
That have scarred the Earth's surface for a lifetime,
Like an ugly black tattoo.
These same beasts crunch away ear-splittingly
In the once silent and peaceful rainforests, the lungs of the Earth.

At the end of my flight I settle down for the night,
Tuck my head under my wing and try to block out
The banging of the bins, sobbing of the homeless and the cries
                                        of the sirens.
That's when I wonder, what would the world look like with
                              the clock turned back?

Emma Todd (13)
John O'Gaunt School, Hungerford

The Clean Earth To The Dirty

Stop it now,
Don't be a know how,
If nothing can be done,
Think of the sun.

Start using electric cars,
Together we can save the moon and the stars.
Temperatures turning hot and cold,
People young and old.

Think of them, do some recycling
Do that and you are doing a good thing.
Rainforests are coming down
To make stuff for cities and towns.

Think of the power plants,
Think of the tiny little ants,
They are important to our eco-system,
Use electric cars and we will save them.

All the poverty in the world,
Try and stop it, spread the word.
If you do this simple deed,
The plants will have good soil to seed.

Holly Thorne (13)
John O'Gaunt School, Hungerford

The Real World

Perfumed pink flowers, what a wonderful world.
Glowing green trees
Swaying in the breeze.
I walked down the road and saw people smile,
I walked for a mile,
But then I froze.

The flowers disappeared; it was grey all around,
There were only five trees
And I couldn't feel the breeze.
I continued, faster, but smiles were now frowns,
Villages were towns,
A world of concrete.

All I saw was rubbish and litter on the streets,
Not a single tree.
So help me please!
I want to see it clean, with flowers all around,
It's time to turn these frowns
The right way round.

Becky Horne (13)
John O'Gaunt School, Hungerford

The Future

Rainforests will not be around,
When people keep chopping trees to the ground.
Boxes, books, paper and board,
People would be moaning, 'Oh Lord, oh Lord.'
When people are depressed and the world is in a mess,
People will shout in stress.
You knew 200 years of chopping and sawing
Would leave us in a mess,
So don't be surprised, it's your problem now,
We're all going to die.

Jimmy Grainger & James Neill-Tadman (12)
Kemnal Technology College, Sidcup

Environment Poem

E njoy all the rabbits while you can
N otice that they will no longer be there
V iews are going to be ruined
I think we should look after the environment
R emember to look after your world
O ne day the ice may all melt
N o one will be able to stop it
M any animals need your help
E veryone can stop it from happening
N ote that we are destroying the Earth
T urn off your TV when you're not watching it,
                    to cut down on electricity.

Keeley Wheatley (12)
Oakmeeds Community College, Burgess Hill

Environment Poem

Environment, environment, what can we do
To save the planet and the ozone too?
Recycle plastic, recycle paper,
So you won't be a resource waster.
Use the sun for heating, the wind for power,
Then we will save the tree and the flower.
Environment, environment, what can you do?
Do all these things and the Earth will renew.

Kelly Gregory (12)
Oakmeeds Community College, Burgess Hill

Our Planet

The trees sway like a lady dancing in the gold wheat fields
And when the grass is shimmering with light from the rain
You can almost see all of the moon in the centre of the grass,
But if we destroy our planet this will never last!
Some people walk and some decide to drive,
We all have our own opinions so that's just how it will go,
But if we take too long to decide, then will our planet ever survive?
As animals would say, is it a bird, is it a plane?
No, it is a construction building!
Run!
So how would you feel if your house was to be built upon?
Please help the animals, save their homes and be their friend
Because enemies do not get along!
Save our planet *now!*

Katie Howard
Oakmeeds Community College, Burgess Hill

My Hope

People farm wind high up on the hills,
Hoping the council will not want to build.
People who care try to be green as the grass,
But some folk think caring is only a farce.
Some people think solar's the best,
But good luck in getting planning permission first.
Some people try to make eco inventions,
But their ideas end up nothing like their intentions.
The world we live in is getting hotter every day
And all some people do is sit there and bathe.
We need to start thinking of a plan
To save our world, I hope that we can.

Eddie Marshall (12)
Oakmeeds Community College, Burgess Hill

Help Save Our Environment

K eeping the environment clean is very important to me
E verybody walk to school, it is good for you and you won't
                              be polluting the atmosphere
E nergy efficient light bulbs are the ones
P lease keep the world clean and tidy

T he world is in a terrible state so you can help us sort it out
H otter and hotter the world is becoming
E verybody can help to make our world a better place

E very time you brush your teeth, always turn the tap off
N ever throw litter
V alue the world
I ntelligent people pick up their litter
R emember to recycle all you can
O nly use the car when necessary
N ever drive if you can walk
M ake something out of recycled things
E nergy is being wasted so try to use it wisely
N o one should ever think about harming the environment
T he world is getting hotter by the minute

C ompost vegetable peelings for your garden
L ight is being wasted
E nergy needs to be saved by turning the lights off when not in use
A lways put your rubbish in the bin
N obody should damage the world.

Lucy Bennet (12)
Oakmeeds Community College, Burgess Hill

The Environment

The mountains, countryside, the wonderful seas,
But the modern world is so bad that
For the environment it's just ifs, buts and maybes.

The jungle, forest, those huge meadows,
But the modern world is so bad that
We pollute the world more than our ancient fellows.

The oceans, rivers, those shimmering lakes,
But the modern world is so bad that
The environment is becoming a world of fakes.

The skies, highs, the transforming weather,
But the modern world is so bad that
It will soon begin to change our lives forever.

The summer, autumn, winter and spring,
But the modern world is so bad that
Who knows what changes these seasons will bring?

Charlie Owen (12)
Oakmeeds Community College, Burgess Hill

Environment Poem

I wish . . .
The grass was greener
And the sky wasn't so grey,
The clouds would be much higher
And we wouldn't have to pay
For the damage we have done,
We'd be happier today,
We wouldn't have to lay
In bed, so sad and worried
About how we can stop
Global warming coming.

Shannon Bowles
Oakmeeds Community College, Burgess Hill

Beautiful Nature!

I'm sitting quietly in this field
Looking all around,
When suddenly jumps out at me
A rabbit from the ground.
It looks around from left to right
While I don't move an inch.
It turns around to look and see,
I know I mustn't flinch.
One, then two, then three, then four,
Hopping out their burrow,
Nature all around me.
I'll be back tomorrow.

Rebecca Wilson (12)
Oakmeeds Community College, Burgess Hill

Environment Poem

E is for environment that we are all destroying!
N is for nuts that are for the squirrels; if we don't feed them
                                                                                  they will die!
V is for very bad environment that we all need to change!
I is for intelligent people that try to make the world
                                                                                   a better place!
R is for rubbish that we must recycle!
O is for the ozone layer that we are destroying
N is for the new life we need to lead
M is for men that clean up the environment
E is for everything that we must recycle!
N is for nothing that will not go to waste!
T is for trees that we must not cut down!

Ben McCreadie
Oakmeeds Community College, Burgess Hill

Environment Poem

The environment
That we don't care about,
The ice caps are melting, polar bears are dying. But we're OK.
Waters are rising, people are dying. But I'm OK.
Trees are falling, oxygen is dying. But I'm OK.
We're all using aerosols, our ozone is dying. But I'm OK.
The chimneys are smoking, the smog is strangling. But I'm OK.
The planet is dying,
I don't feel so good, I can't breathe,
But we still don't care.

But I do care,
I don't want the planet to die.
I do my bit, but is it enough?
I turn of my lights, because I care.
I recycle my waste, because I care.
I walk, don't drive, because I care.
I grow my own food, because I care.
I don't want the planet to die.
I don't want to die. I care.

Vicki Wootten (12)
Oakmeeds Community College, Burgess Hill

Stormy Skies

Dream of our lonely soldier
Strolling down the misty stream.
Lies and deception
Make our new reality.

Our leaders and their freelance words
Create a life we could have had,
Cut from our instincts,
All we see is our pre-made path.

We should never be afraid,
We are protected from trouble and pain,
Then why is this a crisis
In their eyes again?

How did this come to be?
Tied to an endless road,
No love to set us free.
Watch our souls fade away
While our bodies crumble down.
Let's not be afraid
To take my world from you.

And I have recurring nightmares
That I was loved for who I am.
All of the suffering
Could never make for a better man.

Josh King (18)
St Edmund's Catholic School, Dover

The Change

Silently, unaware, the busy world goes by,
Forgotten, mistaken, avoided - they are lies.
Coming, going, but nothing in-between,
Not one spare penny. Not one spare dream.

All hope is spent, washed straight away,
Like that dreadful feeling of having a dire day.
Getting through the weeks and months, without any trouble,
But effect will soon commence and the worries will be double.

It may all sound unreal. It may all sound untrue,
But you cannot begin to know, until you've heard it too.
You've seen it in those movies, you think you've got a feel,
But none of you will understand until you see it for real.

Shattered, broken - a genuine outcast.
So come on, get up, let's put it in the past.
Whichever way you see, it's never going to change,
Unless we all get into gear and tell the world to rearrange.

If you could just imagine, let all thoughts be provoked,
Then I am almost certain you would think and re-look.
For you and me, we are the light; the generation to set them free.
Nobody said it would be easy, but challenge is the key!

These people are real, oh yes they are,
But we have yet to see
That we could change the entire world
If we acted against poverty!

William Hall (12)
St John's Beaumont School, Old Windsor

The Planet

T he planet is the place that we live in,
   That's why you should use the recycling bin!
H omeless people have no space,
   Helpless people are a disgrace!
E ven the richer ones won't donate,
   Ever thought of being like Bill Gates?

P lease take action, please make haste,
   Planet Earth will turn to paste!
L itter mustn't be thrown around,
   Least of all, on the ground!
A fter recycling that bottle of water,
   Add another or you'll get the slaughter!
N ever think this is all a big joke,
   Not even you, pick up that Coke!
E nd the stress,
   Evade the press!
T he planet is giving you its warning,
   Then see the change in the morning!

Omar Ibrahim (12)
St John's Beaumont School, Old Windsor

Climate Change Is Here

Every day we hear
About how we should fear
Of the changing world
And that the new dawn is near.

Some people care,
Some people don't,
They just want to go on holiday
In a big, fat, boat.

What can I do?
What can you do?
You can recycle your bottles,
So the bin nearly topples!

Don't forget to ride that bike
Instead of using that big old van,
When there should be a ban.
You know you can!

You can make a difference
If you want to,
We all can
And we should make a plan!

So recycle, recycle,
Just like John and Michael!
You have to be keen
If you want to go green!

Gregory Hart (12)
St John's Beaumont School, Old Windsor

Stormy Skies

Dream of our lonely soldier
Strolling down the misty stream.
Lies and deception
Make our new reality.

Our leaders and their freelance words
Create a life we could have had,
Cut from our instincts,
All we see is our pre-made path.

We should never be afraid,
We are protected from trouble and pain,
Then why is this a crisis
In their eyes again?

How did this come to be?
Tied to an endless road,
No love to set us free.
Watch our souls fade away
While our bodies crumble down.
Let's not be afraid
To take my world from you.

And I have recurring nightmares
That I was loved for who I am.
All of the suffering
Could never make for a better man.

Josh King (18)
St Edmund's Catholic School, Dover

The Change

Silently, unaware, the busy world goes by,
Forgotten, mistaken, avoided - they are lies.
Coming, going, but nothing in-between,
Not one spare penny. Not one spare dream.

All hope is spent, washed straight away,
Like that dreadful feeling of having a dire day.
Getting through the weeks and months, without any trouble,
But effect will soon commence and the worries will be double.

It may all sound unreal. It may all sound untrue,
But you cannot begin to know, until you've heard it too.
You've seen it in those movies, you think you've got a feel,
But none of you will understand until you see it for real.

Shattered, broken - a genuine outcast.
So come on, get up, let's put it in the past.
Whichever way you see, it's never going to change,
Unless we all get into gear and tell the world to rearrange.

If you could just imagine, let all thoughts be provoked,
Then I am almost certain you would think and re-look.
For you and me, we are the light; the generation to set them free.
Nobody said it would be easy, but challenge is the key!

These people are real, oh yes they are,
But we have yet to see
That we could change the entire world
If we acted against poverty!

William Hall (12)
St John's Beaumont School, Old Windsor

The Rainforest

When that tree got cut down
Amongst the now deserted fields,
The Earth had a big frown
And although it used all its shields,
It couldn't protect itself from its jaws
And the evil grin of all its saws.
That mean machine ate all the wood,
It ate all it could,
And then it came to be
That where it stood, the saviour came
And poured on it like the heaviest rain.

But now it had gone,
Nothing went on
And for years to come
The destruction still weighed a ton,
And the forest was done.

Richard Spanos (12)
St John's Beaumont School, Old Windsor

Pollution

Please stop pollution,
With your contribution
The world will stay living,
Because you are giving.
You're doing a lot,
Now this is your shot.
Cut down on coal, gas and oil,
Then there will be more soil.
If it's a short ride, go on your bike,
Then you'll know what fresh air feels like.
You're saving the world, now give it your all,
Humans are happy here, please don't let Earth fall.

Holly Claridge (12)
Sir William Ramsay School, High Wycombe

Street Life

My home is dim and dirty,
Filled with people that want to hurt me.
My family and loved ones gone,
As the traffic drone echoes on and on and on.

Pollution and litter surround me,
By now someone must have found me.
You're in the warm
While I'm out in the storm.
Will anyone give me a home?

On the streets live hundreds of people,
Outside each temple and steeple.
I'm not on my own,
But we're all alone.
Will someone give us a home?

Megan Stiles (12)
Sir William Ramsay School, High Wycombe

It's Up To Us

The environment is lacking care,
The environment is here to share.
The Kyoto Protocol didn't work,
Thanks to one particular jerk.
There must be more that we can do,
Looks like it's up to me and you
To change the way we live our lives,
To make sure the human race survives.
If we don't make a stand today,
The world we love will fade away.

Josh Nicholls (11)
Sir William Ramsay School, High Wycombe

Tell Your Family And Your Friends

Tell your family and your friends
To help the planet and farmers' land,
And if we all eventually succeed,
Maybe we won't lose too many of our trees.
Even it it's only one thing,
Saving water or electricity
So we can always hear the birds sing.
Various things can save this land,
Educate your family,
Inform your friends,
Will you do your part to save the planet?
And instead of pollution,
Our world will be cleansed,
So tell your family and your friends.

Louise Church (15)
Thamesview School, Gravesend

Environment

E nvironment rules
N eeds cleaning
V ery badly
I t is important
R eally needs cleaning
O ur environment is dying
N eeds cleaning
M y world smells of smoke
E veryone can try
N o one can't clean
T ry to stop global warming.

Chris Hutchison (13)
Thamesview School, Gravesend

What Do You See?

When you gaze into the stars, what do you see?
Do you see happiness, wealth and tranquillity?
Or do you see pain, torture and poverty?

When you gaze in the sky on a clear sunny day, what do you see?
Do you see shelter, water and much to eat?
Or do you see mud huts, dirty water and little food?

When you gaze out to sea, what do you see?
Do you see mildness, self-control and peace?
Or do you see anger, violence and men that are beasts?

When you lie on a bed of grass, what do you see?
Do you see goodness, faith and long-suffering?
Or do you see evil, wars and the 'us or them' attitude?

When you walk through the forest, what do you see?
Do you see health, life and happy families?
Or do you see illness, hatred. Please tell me what you see.

Just tell me what you see!

Taylor Barnard (13)
The Brakenhale School, Bracknell

Reuse, Recycle, Reduce

Make the world a better place,
Reuse, recycle, reduce.
When you recycle old things,
New ones can be produced.

Don't make the world worse than it is,
Save the animals,
Save the trees,
Don't pollute the rivers or the seas.

Walk to school,
Don't use your car,
Walk to the shops,
It can't be that far!

Zoe Tate (12)
The Matthew Arnold School, Staines

Reduce

R euse, recycle, reduce your rubbish
E veryone can help
D on't pollute your universe
U se your stuff more than once
C ans, tins and bags can be recycled too
E verything can make something new.

Shannen Fisher (12)
The Matthew Arnold School, Staines

The World

The world is a disgrace,
I cannot think
Of how we humans,
Can make our homes stink.

We have to make a change,
We can all take part,
The time is running out,
So let's make a start.

Cutting down on gas,
And other fossil fuels,
Recycling is another thing,
But you haven't see it all!

Animals are dying,
So are the trees and plants,
We can't live without them,
And we only have one chance.

If we start making a difference,
The world will be great,
Because if we don't,
Our lives will be at stake.

Nancy Berry (12)
The Matthew Arnold School, Staines

Recycle Now

Recycle now,
Save the Earth,
Don't care how,
For all it's worth.

Save the land,
Don't concrete over,
Make a garden,
From what's left over.

Save the forest,
From being chopped down,
Help the monkeys,
Don't watch and frown.

Daniel Morris (12)
The Matthew Arnold School, Staines

Pollution

Don't drive so much,
Walk a lot more,
Kill nuclear, start solar,
Less pollution, we're killing the world,
The greenhouse gases are melting the ice caps.

Rory Carroll (12)
The Matthew Arnold School, Staines

Recycle Please

You may die if you don't recycle,
So save the world, protect the world,
If you don't recycle
You could kill the world,
So recycle please,
And yes, this means you!

Jack Smith (13)
The Matthew Arnold School, Staines

Recycling

Cut down on rubbish to save the land,
Recycling is giving the world a hand.
Do the wildlife a big favour,
Recycle lots and lots of paper.
If you walk instead of drive,
You will keep nature alive.
If we don't cut the trees down,
It will rewind our environment and town.
If we recycle all together,
We can save the Earth for ever and ever!

Harriet Goodger (12)
The Matthew Arnold School, Staines

A Better Place

I want the world to be a better place,
With rubbish thrown away.
Respect the animals that live with us,
They might thank us one day.

Remember when you drop litter
How many things could be affected
In ways not to be shown.

So walk or ride
To save the world,
Not to pollute the streets we live in.

Harvey Parsons (12)
The Matthew Arnold School, Staines

Recycle

Recycle,
Don't put it in the bin.
Recycle,
Reuse that old tin.

When you use paper,
Use both sides,
It will save trees,
That's no lie.

Stop cutting down
Rainforest trees,
They bring life
To birds and bees.

Car pool to save petrol,
Or ride a bike to school.
You could take a bus
Or walk to the pool.

Act now,
It's important, right?
You could recycle
Or turn off the light.

Chris Cook (12)
The Matthew Arnold School, Staines

Pollution - Haiku

Makes global warming
Mainly made by fossil fuels
And greenhouse gases.

Frankie Brown (12)
The Matthew Arnold School, Staines

Extinction

Extinction leaves the planet bare,
Without a trace of pheasant or hare.
No one can imagine what it would be like,
Without a stingray, cod fish or pike.

Humans are greedy, powerful, obstructive,
But they can be rich, clever and constructive.
Why can't they see, before it's too late,
And pull nature out of this miserable fate?

Jonathan Wells (12)
The Matthew Arnold School, Staines

Do It Now!

We should take care of our world,
Our world is very special.
Recycle and save all the time.
Little is a lot.
Do it now!

Rachel Hall (12)
The Matthew Arnold School, Staines

Remember To Recycle

R emember to recycle
E very little helps
C ardboard boxes
Y our milk bottle will do
C ome on, guys
L et's recycle
I need your help
N ow! To make a better place
G et going, be green!

Lily Butler (13)
The Matthew Arnold School, Staines

Recycling

R educing the consumption of fresh raw materials
E nergy usages are reduced
C lears streets
Y ou recycle with the aim of preventing the waste
C leans the environment
L owering greenhouse gas
I ncludes glass, paper, metal, textiles and plastics
N ot leaving your rubbish all around
G reen bins.

Zoe High (13)
The Matthew Arnold School, Staines

The Environment - Haiku

The environment
Is getting really dirty.
We need to clean it.

Lauren Griffin (12)
The Matthew Arnold School, Staines

Recycling

R ecycling is fun
E nvironment-friendly
C ardboard and plastics
Y oghurt pots and bottles
C ans and tins
L ive in recycling bins
I nto composting
N ever forget, so . . .
G et recycling!

Leanne Barnes & Kerry Bunston (12)
The Matthew Arnold School, Staines

Litter

Litter can be a mess,
Litter can be smelly,
Litter can be a load of clutter,
Litter can be dirty,
If you recycle your litter it's for the best!

Litter can be untidy,
Litter can be scraps,
Litter can be junk,
Litter can be trash,
Start recycling your litter, you will be the best.

Litter is rubbish,
Litter can be bits and pieces,
Litter is garbage,
Litter can be odds and ends,
If you recycle your litter, things will be cheaper.

Trish Bangezhano (12)
The Radcliffe School, Wolverton

In Africa . . .

In Africa you can go and see
Zebras, lions and rhinos.
In Africa you can also see
Hunger, thirst and death.
Malawi, Sudan and Kenya
Are just some of the places it happens,
But we can do something about this
And help the people who need us.
By working together and raising money
These people can get what they need to live.

Hannah Greig (14)
The Radcliffe School, Wolverton

Why Drop It?

When you have a bite to eat,
Could be a wrapper from a sweet,
Could be a bottle, or could be a treat,
But why chuck it in the street?

Could be a can or could be a packet,
Could be paper or could be plastic,
Could be a tin or could be some bar,
Put it in the bin, it can't be far.

So next time you drop it,
Think . . . I'd hate to mop it,
I may as well stop it.

Joe Bulman (13)
The Radcliffe School, Wolverton

Peace!

Pollution is taking over the Earth,
Millions malnourished at birth.

Help them now,
Before it's too late.
Talk about it,
Even with a mate.

Take action,
Take control,
Even something small
Can take a role.

In the streets
Or in your home,
In Paris
Or even Rome.

Starving children . . .
Do you feel bad?
Yet we still fight wars,
Now that makes me mad!

Kerry Clarke (14)
The Radcliffe School, Wolverton

Penguin Having His Say!

They say humans are better than us,
But we don't need to use a train or a bus.
My name is Pete Penguin,
And soon I will die.
Please let me live, don't make me cry.

If you help me
I'll be the greatest as can be.
Turn off the telly, stop the world being smelly.
Make me happy, I'm Pete,
Make my life sweet.

It's all because of you
Leaving litter, crap and poo.
Polar bear is getting angry,
If you don't act, we'll create a pact.
Save me, let me be free!

Matthew Rogers (13)
The Radcliffe School, Wolverton

Homeless People

They can't help the way they are,
They really need help,
They can't even drive a car.
They give a big yelp
For someone to help,
So here we are.
That's just the way they are.

Kelsie Griffin (13)
The Radcliffe School, Wolverton

What Have We Become? - Haikus

Guns, planes are coming,
There is nothing we can do,
Except quiver with fear . . .

The siren is loud,
Blaring out to take cover;
Many shall survive.

We could have stopped this;
Destroying all of the bombs,
Make this place happy.

Yet the gas rises,
Slowly till it covers me
And I suffocate.

We shall rise again
And strike back from our cities;
Preparing to fight.

We shall strike their plants,
Destroying their towns and homes,
Killing their soldiers.

We're destroying them!
We're stooping to their level . . .
What have we become?

Jake Munn (14)
The Radcliffe School, Wolverton

We Need Your Help

People have stopped caring,
I don't know why.
Animals and rainforests
Are all going to die.

We're changing our world,
But not for the better,
Our winters are warmer
And our summers are wetter.

The temperature is changing,
We just can't wait,
There isn't time,
We know our fate.

You have to help
To prevent a war
Between us and nature,
You could do more.

Recycle your rubbish,
Reduce your trash,
If you do your bit,
It could be gone in a flash.

People think it doesn't matter
But you could help,
Together we could change the future.

Eleanor Gregory (12)
The Radcliffe School, Wolverton

It's In Our Nature To Destroy Ourselves

War has broken loose,
The horn is getting louder,
People outside factories
Stacking crates of gunpowder.

Stupid government nitwits
Wasting all our funds,
Striving for control,
Buying all these guns.

Soldiers lying everywhere
On the brink of death,
Then in an instant,
They take their final breath.

War is the worst place to be
When you don't know what to do,
Trying to escape it,
Struggling to make it through.

The gas is now rising,
The shrapnel falling down,
There is now nothing left
Of what once was a town.

The world is hanging by a thread,
Forever, it shall not cope,
Our final hour has almost come . . .
Was there ever any hope?

Daniel Jones (14)
The Radcliffe School, Wolverton

We Die At Our Own Hands

The planet gives us all we need,
But asks for nothing in return.
We eat and drink and always breathe,
So why won't people learn?

You kick, chuck and drop your litter
And think nothing of the crime,
But when it comes to your money,
You don't like to pay the fine.

You hunt down many animals
Of beauty and splendour,
But they'll eventually disappear,
Because there's no defender.

You have to help your planet
From such horrible, cruel things,
This message must be heard
So in your ear it rings.

It is OK for a luxury
Every now and then,
But if you get too greedy,
I'll read this poem again.

Ceejay Stewart (13)
The Radcliffe School, Wolverton

Homeless People

All around the world are people on the streets,
Drinking, eating, sleeping, sitting and laying,
That is what they put up with.
On the streets, there every day,
Trying to live and not to die.
They're always alone, no one to hold,
But when they are held, they will be loved.
They find things difficult: eating and drinking,
Finding the warmth with a bit of tinkering.
They'll find help, with a bit of love,
But if they don't, have some hope.

Ryan Murphy (13)
The Radcliffe School, Wolverton

War, War

War, war everywhere,
Spreading fear everywhere.
People crying and running away
As gunfire ruins the day.
Planes in the air dropping bombs
And polluting the air,
Children playing around;
As bullets hit, they fall to the ground.
Enemy approaching from all around,
People who are scared lie on the ground.
People praying for mercy
As people die all around.
People living off the land,
People destroying it on demand.
War, war is a terrible thing,
People suffer, poor things.

Rachel Baker (12)
The Radcliffe School, Wolverton

A World We Live In

Our world is a big messy place,
Could do with being cleaned up,
So nothing goes to waste.

There is the environment,
Animals and extinction too.
If we were not doing this, would it be you?

Help us so that nothing will suffer.
Help us so that we can clean up the damage
That has been caused.

Come and help us, do not sit back and pause.
If we don't do this now,
The world will be turned upside down.

It will never be able to be turned around.
So come on, come and help us
So that we can change the whole wide world.

Lauren Kemp (12)
The Radcliffe School, Wolverton

The Streets

On the streets . . .
There they stay,
Begging for money
To feed the next day.

On the streets . . .
There they lay
In the cold, wind and rain.

Help them through,
This is down to you.
Help them through,
It's down to you!

Melanie Small (14)
The Radcliffe School, Wolverton

My War Poem

This is a poem about war,
People who are getting really sore.
They kill the poor
Just for the war.

There are people dying in the night,
Even though it doesn't serve them right.
They battle for their glory gold,
Even as foretold.

Planes, planes in the air,
Dropping bombs and polluting the air.
Planes, planes in the air,
Flying proudly through the air.

Child by child sitting down,
As they fall to the ground,
People here and there,
Falling through the dusty air.

Gun by gun shooting there and there,
People running like a hare,
People proud around the world,
Unlike others on the other side of the world.

Josh Davey (12)
The Radcliffe School, Wolverton

Beware The Hunters

Here come the hunters ready to poach,
Trying to swat a scared cockroach.
Finding the animals on their map,
Setting a giant bear trap.
They like to strike in the middle of the night
Because that's when they cause the most fright.
Baby deer lying in a field,
Not knowing they will soon be killed.
Every day someone hurts a bear.
Please people, try to care!

Dean Joce (13)
The Radcliffe School, Wolverton

Save The Planet

S ave the planet like a babysitter
A nimal extinction is happening because of our litter
V alley of flowers, all red and green
E lephants shouted across the stream

T hink, think before you pollute
H elp the planet and salute
E nvironments are being destroyed

P ollution's being caused by our own toys
L ove the planet, love the beautiful environment,
                stop polluting before it's destroyed
A nimals are becoming extinct by chopping down the trees
N o, no, no, please stop! Otherwise there will not be any breeze
E arth is filled with people who are homeless
T ired and hungry, but helpless.

Amarah Saleem (12)
The Radcliffe School, Wolverton

The War And The Boys

'Fight, fight!' children shout.
One punch, two punches, fists are flying.
Teachers come out shouting, 'Stop, stop!
Get back to class, you 'orrible lot!'
'Aww, Miss!' they mumble under their breath,
Two young boys standing instead!
First boy standing with bruises on his face,
Second boy, not a cut or a grace.
Which one's the bully,
Can you guess?
This is war, it's not the best!

George Janes (12)
The Radcliffe School, Wolverton

The Word Destruction Tour

Bang! This is what we hear when we see a tree falling.
Bang! This is what we hear when people make careless money.
The Earth is dying, the money is defying,
People killing, but so very willing.
Animals lose homes and hope as people do this to our rainforests.
Animals wiped out as well as the smile on our faces.
We cry and try, but nothing comes of it.
The government's defying, not helping one bit,
Front page things ignored by all.
This is everybody's will but still it is forgotten.
Animals' families killed and forgotten.
This truly is a world destruction tour.

Peter Downing (12)
The Radcliffe School, Wolverton

Litter And Homeless

When you drop litter,
The animals will have no homes to live in.
If they have no homes to live in
They will die.
If you don't drop litter,
The animals will not pass away.
They will have a home to live in
If you put a single bit of litter in the bin.
You are saving the environment.
When you save the environment,
You are saving the world.

Chantelle Stubbings (12)
The Radcliffe School, Wolverton

Green And Clean

Being great and green
Will keep your environment clean.
Recycling is good,
So help clean your neighbourhood.
Help clean the river,
So the fish can swim through,
If you do,
The animals will love you.

Tom Compton (13)
The Radcliffe School, Wolverton

Litter

Litter destroys the world,
Thrown on the ground, kicked around the fields,
The environment looks dirty,
Litter makes it smelly.

By cleaning up the litter,
The environment is clean, the atmosphere feels fresher,
So pick up some rubbish, throw it in the bin,
So the world feels just a bit more clean.

Megan Duke (13)
The Radcliffe School, Wolverton

Recycling

You are making this country a mess,
All you have to do is put your litter in the bin.
If you do, you will make this world a better place.
If you don't, you will make it a disgrace.
So all we're asking is just for you to put your litter in the bin.
Loads of people, pets are suffering because of litter.
What could you have done?
Put your litter in the bin.

Taylor Hamilton (11)
The Radcliffe School, Wolverton

Help

Some people you have to let go,
It's hard, don't worry, I know.
Yes we can help out I say,
We can help plants and trees,
Not by begging on our knees.
So why can't we help other things too
At war is very scary.
Monkeys are really quite hairy!
So why not help out,
With a scream or a shout,
To help us clean up all these things?
Help the animals,
Help the trees,
Help the environment,
Please, please, please,
Help!

Shannon Weir (12)
The Radcliffe School, Wolverton

The Green World!

We must protect our trees
Just like we protect our Queen.
The wild should live,
Not get blown adrift.
Your garden should get planted
And not get shunted.
Keep your dog on a lead
But don't let it run off to read.
Don't damage plants for the animals to feed,
You'll just make them plead.
Don't use a car
If you're not going that far.
Do this to give the world some more time
And then maybe I'll give you a piece of lime.

EJ Cooper
The Radcliffe School, Wolverton

Being Homeless

B egging for money
E ager for food
I solated, on your own
N o one else around you
G etting more ill by the second

H oping someone will help but all that will happen is
O nly going to be horrible
M ean people will pass you and say,
'E ww, what a dirty tramp' or words to that effect
L isten here, just ignore them
E ven though you can hear them. Just think how they would
                              feel in your position.
S o now you can have a nice, soothing night's sleep
S *ave the homeless!* Think about how they feel, for once!

So what are you going to do?

Jadine Lane (11)
The Radcliffe School, Wolverton

Be Green, Be Clean, Be A Hero And Save The Earth!

Be a helping hand
To save this Earth.
Remember the three Rs?
Reduce, reuse and recycle!
Don't pollute now,
One person could change this planet.
We need you.
When you're in your room in the daytime
Do you really need your light on?
Protect this planet, before it's too late!

Laura Beaton (12)
The Radcliffe School, Wolverton

Why?

People are dying, why?
There is war, why?
Extinct animals, why?
Poverty everywhere, why?
Refugees, why?
Trees and plants dying, why?
Help the world.

Imagine what it is gong to be like;
No food, no water, no fuel,
No money, no family and no *you*.
There might not be an Earth,
Just an empty planet with water
And a few islands and no one there.

So help me, help you, by saving our world.
If we don't act soon,
Our lives will be cut short
And no one wants that

Think!
The world is in our hands!

Ronica Nyarirangwe (11)
The Radcliffe School, Wolverton

Animals Here And There!

Animals, animals here and there,
Animals, animals everywhere.
In people's homes, out in the wild,
Animals, animals wherever you go,
Animals, animals with nothing to eat,
No trees, no leaves for a feast!

Chelcie Addis (12)
The Radcliffe School, Wolverton

My Green Poem

Our home is the world,
So we must protect its precious load.
The trees cry
As they fall and die.

Don't put cereal boxes in the bin, recycle.
Don't take the car, cycle.
Take the train,
Rather than the plane.

Don't litter,
It makes you quite bitter.
Turn the lights off
And become like a boff.

Save the trees,
Please.

Luke Turner (12)
The Radcliffe School, Wolverton

A Greener Planet

Help the planet, make it cleaner,
This will make the world much greener.
You can recycle your plastics
Recycle your glass,
That will reduce greenhouse gas.
Reduce your spray,
Reduce the ray,
Try not to use much hair mousse
Each and every day.
Cycle or walk,
But don't take the bus
Because you don't want to make a fuss.

Matthew Downs (12)
The Radcliffe School, Wolverton

The Green Thing

Oh what a waste
Throwing it away,
Save it, store it,
To use another day.

Recycling, recycling,
Please think before
You put it in the bin.

Will it be used by another,
Or crushed or melted away?
Made into something new
For us to use again?

Metal, glass, paper and string
Can become new books, bottles,
Cans, cars and many other new things.

New from old will help to save
The world in which we live.
To save the trees, recycle please,
Our world is getting tired.

Tom Lawrence (12)
The Radcliffe School, Wolverton

Planet Green

Green is our planet,
Full of trees, grass, plants and hope,
So don't turn it grey with pollution,
Don't be a dope.

Joshua McMillan (12)
The Radcliffe School, Wolverton

Save The Planet

S is for save the planet
A is for all work together
V is for very special
E is for everyone unite

T is for together we can do it
H is for help us save the world
E is for excellent work

P is for poorly planet
L is for love the Earth
A is for amazing success
N is for never give up
E is for elephants and other animals
T is for today.

Emily Boycott
The Radcliffe School, Wolverton

The World

In this world everything's going wrong.
The sea is ready to take us all
And we are the ones destroying nature,
We are killing the air on this tiny little planet.

We are killing the world we love.
I love this planet, now my hope is fading away,
But are you ready to make a difference?
Please take care of our precious planet.

Jamie King (12)
The Radcliffe School, Wolverton

What Would I Do If I Could Save The World?

What would I do if I could save the world?

First I would save the forests
I would stop people cutting them down
So all the tribes and animals
Could smile and not frown

Then I would save the penguins
With their little fluffy feathers
I would save them
From the Antarctic's warming weathers.

After that I might
Give children cleaner water
The rivers are so dirty
It's like sending them for slaughter

Next, what would I save?
The ozone layer, oh yes!
I would get it out of its current state
It's shamble, it's a mess!

Recycling would be my next stop
I'd make people more green
So our amazing planet
Would lose its oily sheen!

Oh what would I do?
If I could make our world pure bliss
Oh what would I do?
I would do *all* of this!

Rachael Banes
The Radcliffe School, Wolverton

Climate Change

C old is more
L ots of heat
I ce is melting
M ammals are affected
A ll because of you
T ogether we can stop it
E veryone will be safe

C aution must be taken
H ow we do this is up to you
A ll this was our fault
N ow let's destroy it
G o on, do it
E veryone can!

Jack Webster (12)
The Radcliffe School, Wolverton

Environment

E veryone
N ever
V isualises
I gloos
R ainforests
O il
N ow CO_2
M oney
E veryone
N ever
T hinks.

Stephen Reilly (12)
The Radcliffe School, Wolverton

Recycling

R ecycling will save the planet
E veryone should do it
C an we save the planet?
Y es we can
C ome, join in too
L iving is everything
I t's not too late but we have to take action
N o one has an excuse
G o on, be proud!

Victoria Hardwick
The Radcliffe School, Wolverton

Trees To Bed

The sky is blue,
The sun is bright,
I used to be tall
Before they took away my height.

I've seen things be born and die,
And although I'm 142 years old,
It only took them seconds
To cut me down.

I think I'm going to be a bed.
You could have tried to help,
But it's too late now . . .
I'm already dead.

Tison Bailey (13)
Woodbridge Park Education Service, Isleworth

The Trees Are Crying

I used to be so proud, so strong, so tall,
That was before they made me too small.
Sounds of death and crying as they stood tall, no more,
Only sounds of fighting as they started to fall.
I had nightmares of the trees beginning to drop,
I begged them, 'Please, please stop hurting me,'
But they wouldn't listen to me.
Now the rainforest is never to be seen
Because of this greed.

Hollie Turner (14)
Woodbridge Park Education Service, Isleworth

Chugging Chimneys

Chimneys standing tall and high,
Fogging out the big blue sky.
The public walking quickly by,
All I can hear is the people sigh.

Killing the birds flying and soaring,
From the front the city looks boring.
Not a pretty sight for those who are touring,
From every chimney smoke is pouring.

I don't agree with the ruined view,
I don't agree with what they do,
Contaminating the skies of blue.
Of all the workers there's only a few
That are left to ruin the public's view.

Taylor O'Brien (13)
Woodbridge Park Education Service, Isleworth

Young Writers Information

We hope you have enjoyed reading this book - and that you will continue to enjoy it in the coming years.

If you like reading and writing poetry drop us a line, or give us a call, and we'll send you a free information pack.

Alternatively if you would like to order further copies of this book or any of our other titles, then please give us a call or log onto our website at www.youngwriters.co.uk

Young Writers Information
Remus House
Coltsfoot Drive
Peterborough
PE2 9JX

(01733) 890066